D1566064

THE ROLE OF PRIVATE FINANCIAL WEALTH IN A PORTFOLIO MODEL

The Role of Private Financial Wealth in a Portfolio Model

A Study of the Effects of Fiscal Deficits on the Real Exchange Rate

Angel Calderón-Madrid

Professor of Macroeconomic Theory and International Economics
El Colegio de Mexico
Mexico City

First published in Great Britain 1995 by
MACMILLAN PRESS LTD
Houndmills, Basingstoke, Hampshire RG21 6XS
and London
Companies and representatives
throughout the world

A catalogue record for this book is available
from the British Library.

ISBN 0–333–62207–3

First published in the United States of America 1995 by
ST. MARTIN'S PRESS, INC.,
Scholarly and Reference Division,
175 Fifth Avenue,
New York, N.Y. 10010

ISBN 0–312–12605–0

Library of Congress Cataloging-in-Publication Data
Calderón-Madrid, Angel.
The role of private financial wealth in a portfolio model : a
study of the effects of fiscal deficits on the real exchange rate /
Angel Calderón-Madrid.
p.   cm.
Based on the author's thesis (Ph.D.)—University of Cambridge,
England.
Includes bibliographical references and index.
ISBN 0–312–12605–0
1. Budget deficits.   2. Fiscal policy.   3. Foreign exchange rates.
4. Debts, Public.   I. Title.
HJ2005.C35   1995
332.4'56—dc20   94–45746
                                                                CIP

© Angel Calderón-Madrid 1995

All rights reserved. No reproduction, copy or transmission of
this publication may be made without written permission.

No paragraph of this publication may be reproduced, copied or
transmitted save with written permission or in accordance with
the provisions of the Copyright, Designs and Patents Act 1988,
or under the terms of any licence permitting limited copying
issued by the Copyright Licensing Agency, 90 Tottenham Court
Road, London W1P 9HE.

Any person who does any unauthorised act in relation to this
publication may be liable to criminal prosecution and civil
claims for damages.

10   9   8   7   6   5   4   3   2   1
04   03   02   01   00   99   98   97   96   95

Printed and bound in Great Britain by
Antony Rowe Ltd, Chippenham, Wiltshire

Contents

Preface   vii

Introduction   ix

1 Long-Run Effects of Fiscal Policy and Domestic Public Debt on the Real Levels of Exchange Rate and GDP   1

Introduction and Summary of Results   1
A Mundell–Fleming Model with a Supply Side   4
   Specification of the Model   4
   Description of the Model   5
Effectiveness of Fiscal Policy in Changing the Level of GDP: the Case of a Downward-flexible Real Wage   11
   Reduced-form Solution   12
   Long-run Multipliers of Public Expenditure on GDP   15
   Foreign Trade Multipliers   18
Effectiveness of fiscal policy to change the level of GDP: The case of real wage rigidity   20
   Equilibrium Solution   21
   Effects on the Level of Exchange Rate   24
   Effects on the Level of GDP   27
Concluding Comments   30

2 The Dynamics of Real Exchange Rate and Financial Assets of Contractionary Fiscal Policies cum Private Dissavings   31

Introduction and Summary of Results   31
A Dynamic Model of the Real Exchange Rate   35
   Specification of the Model   35
   Steady-state Representation   41
   Analysis of the Steady-State Characteristics of the Model   42

Dynamic Analysis Resulting from Private Dissavings
cum Contractionary Fiscal Policies   51
  The Mundell–Fleming Results and the Monotonic
  Convergence Path to the long-run Equilibrium   51
  Impact Exchange Rate Adjustment   53
  A Non-Monotonic Convergence Path   56
  Analysis of the Dynamic Characteristics of the System
  Matrix   61

**3 Stock-Flow Adjustment and the Speed of Convergence
of the Economy towards its Long-Run Equilibrium**   **67**

Introduction and Summary of Results   67
Specification of the Model   70
  Simplifying Assumptions and Policy Rules   70
  Analysis of the Single-Period Structure of the Model   75
  Analysis of the Dynamic Structure of the Model   83
Determinants of the Speed of Adjustment of the
Economy Toward its Long-run Equilibrium   88
  Medium-term Determination of the Level of GDP
  and the Speed of Adjustment of GDP Toward its
  Long-run Equilibrium   89
  Distributed Lag Models and the Dynamic
  Determination of Privately-held Financial Assets   94
  Determinants of the Speed of Convergence of
  Privately held Financial Assets to its Long-run
  Equilibrium Level   97
  Determinants of the Speed of Convergence of the
  Level of GDP to its Long-run Equilibrium   100
  Medium-term Effects of Stocks on the Level of GDP
  and the Overshooting of the Long-run Equilibrium   107
  Stability Conditions   112
Concluding Comments   115

Notes and References   117

Bibliography   121

Index   125

Preface

The atmosphere at the Center of Economics, El Colegio de Mexico, Mexico City, stimulated my work during the years of final preparation of this book. Previous versions of material contained in it were presented at the X, XI and XII meetings of the Latin American Econometric Society (in Argentina, Mexico and Uruguay) where I received other useful comments.

Some of the ideas presented here were first analyzed in my PhD dissertation written at the University of Cambridge, England. The suggestions made by my examiners, William Buiter of Yale University and Wynne Godley of Cambridge University, encouraged me to further develop them.

My greatest debt in this effort is to Professor, now Lord, Desai of the London School of Economics, who patiently read parts of my work and enriched them with his stimulating discussions. I am also indebted to Martin Weale, Hashem Pesaran and Ken Coutts of Cambridge University. Last, but not least, my thanks go to my colleagues and graduate students at El Colegio de Mexico, who also provided useful suggestions on improving the presentation of the ideas contained in this book.

Angel Calderón-Madrid

Introduction

Our theoretical starting point is the modern reformulated version of the Mundell–Fleming approach to an open economy. A quarter century after the foundation of this framework, Frenkel and Razin (1987) refer to it as the 'work horse' of traditional open-economy macroeconomics. The results associated with this framework concerning the effects of fiscal policy in a flexible exchange rate regime are the main, but not the exclusive concern of our study.

One of the most enduring propositions of this approach is that a change in fiscal policy induces a movement in the real exchange rate, which yields an offsetting change in the trade balance. We consider this proposition and ask how its robustness is qualified when changes in the level of domestic public debt and in the amount of private financial wealth enter into the analysis.

In one part of our work we analyze the way in which this proposition must be reformulated to include a long-run requirement, that is, that net exports must compensate for cumulative changes in interest earnings on foreign assets, occurring as a consequence of the cumulative sum of current account imbalances induced by fiscal actions.

The intrinsic dynamics of modern versions of the Mundell–Fleming model are constituted on the one hand by forward-looking expectations of exchange rate movements and on the other by stock-flow adjustments of assets towards a long-run equilibrium. These components constitute a key element in the dynamic analysis of our work and are the basis of some of the questions addressed here.

In a model with a flexible exchange rate, in which fiscal imbalances are allowed to change the level of domestic public indebtedness, we consider the implications for the dynamics of the exchange rate and private financial wealth of a macroeconomic scenario that is not contemplated by the conventional Mundell–Fleming analysis.

This is when an initial phase of the dynamic trajectory of the economy is characterized by reductions in fiscal deficits that are accompanied by more-than-compensating reductions in private surplus, thereby exhibiting privately financed current account deficits and an exchange rate appreciated with respect to its predisturbance level.

What makes this case particularly interesting is that it raises the possibility of a trajectory characterized by alternating sequences of deficits and surplus in the current account of the balance of payments.

With a constant level of GDP, the combination of the use of fiscal instruments and the postulated behavior by the private sector requires a non-monotonic movement of the exchange rate. That is, an initial appreciation followed by a depreciation and a final exchange rate appreciation.

In models with forward-looking expectations of exchange rate movements, it is a common procedure to rely on a dynamic structure that rules out, by construction, a non-monotonic behavior of the system. In this book we study this case in an analytically tractable model, thereby gaining insight into the functioning and required extensions of the modern version of a stock-flow model within the Mundell–Fleming tradition.

In stock-flow models such as the ones presented here, the changes in the level of stocks are a driving force leading the economy from a predisturbance situation to a new long-run equilibrium.

In another part of this book we show that, by exploiting the restrictions that the stock adjustment mechanism places on the lag relations among the flow variables, it is possible to deduce indicators of the speed of adjustment of the system toward a long-run equilibrium.

Our analysis highlights the importance that adjustments in the stock of privately held financial assets have for the determination and speed of medium-run effects of shocks to the economy. It also yields a number of insights into the characteristics of the convergence path of a stock-flow model with an endogenous level of GDP.

Based on the consistency in the stock and flow relationships that characterize these models, we deduce and interpret analytical results about variations in the equilibrium level of GDP and financial assets that are not exclusively related to the short- and long-run effects of a shock to the system.

We provide a framework for considering the proposition that the mean lag of the long-run response of GDP to a permanent change in the level of either public expenditure or exports is determined by the steady-state ratio of the level of the net stock of privately held financial assets to the level of the autonomous component of aggregate demand.

These results are achieved by combining conventional dynamic analysis with a further procedure, which is to restate its dynamic structure as a distributed lag model solving for the equilibrium level of the stock of privately held financial assets. We illustrate the utility of this procedure for a better understanding of the determinants of the convergence path of the economy to a new long-run equilibrium.

AN OVERVIEW OF THE BOOK

This work is divided into three large, self-contained chapters, each of which develops a particular point at the expense of simplifying aspects that constitute the focus of our attention in the other chapters.

For example, the second chapter concentrates on the dynamic implications of forward-looking expectations about exchange rate movements, whereas the third highlights results linked to dynamic stock-flow adjustments in a macroeconomic model.

The material presented in Chapter 1 is not a dynamic analysis. Its objective is to highlight issues that can be addressed by concentrating exclusively on the long-run equilibrium of a portfolio model for a small, open economy.

There we include a supply-side relationship in order to consider the role played by different assumptions about flexibility of real wages, to determine the relationship between expansionary fiscal policies and the level of GDP. With this framework we are able to highlight cases of incompatibility of the structure of the model with the postulate contained in the Mundell–Fleming approach, according to which the level of public expenditure can be considered as an exogenously determined variable.

In Chapter 2 we present a model whose steady state has two properties shared by the framework of Chapter 1. First, as in the paper by Dornbusch and Fischer (1980), the levels of real exchange rate and of net private sector holdings of foreign assets are inversely related across steady states. Second, variations in the level of domestic public debt are related to changes in the real level of the exchange rate: as in the work by Sachs and Wyplosz (1984), we allow fiscal imbalances to change the level of domestic public indebtedness and consider the implications for exchange rate dynamics.

Due to these peculiarities of the model we have, at the outset, the following two implications embedded in our analysis. On the one hand, stating that a long-run decrease in the real level of the accumulated sum of domestically-financed fiscal deficits – that is, the level of domestic public indebtedness – is perceived as feasible by the private sector, is tantamount to stating that a long-run real exchange rate appreciation is expected to take place. On the other hand, if *ex hypothesis* short-run private sector dissavings more than compensate for public sector savings, then an initial exchange rate appreciation must occur for the implied current account deficit to be registered.

These two implications, in turn, generate the following question: how can both a short- and long-run real exchange rate appreciation be possible, given the constraint requiring that long-run variations in interest earnings on foreign assets, resulting from a different net foreign asset position of the economy, be matched with net exports at a post-disturbance steady state?

The answer to this question, to be explored in Chapter 2, is that the exchange rate must follow a dynamic trajectory so as to enable a sequence of current account deficits to be more than compensated by a sequence of current account surpluses.

Whenever the real exchange rate is below its predisturbance level the current account is in deficit and, consequently, a reduction in the level of foreign assets held by the private sector takes place. Since a long-run exchange rate appreciation is associated with a net level of foreign assets at the new steady state, higher than its predisturbance level, there must necessarily be an eventual reversal of the movement in the level of foreign assets during the transition to the long-run. For these reversals to occur, the convergence path of the real exchange rate must be non-monotonic, thereby enabling changes in the level of foreign assets owing to a sequence of current account surpluses to be larger than the absolute value of the change in assets owing to current account deficits.

Finally, in Chapter 3 the analysis focuses on the importance that adjustments in the stock of privately held financial assets has for the determination and speed of medium-run effects of shocks to the economy. It enables us to straddle the gap between interpreting short-, medium- and long-run multiplier effects that autonomous changes in aggregate demand have on the level of GDP and on other endogenous variables of the model.

Unlike the fixed level of GDP models associated with the monetary approach to the balance of payments, the framework presented here stresses the importance of stock adjustment processes in a context in which the levels of assets desired by the private sector depend on scale variables that change throughout the transition to a new long-run equilibrium.

Since some of the indicators of the speed of adjustment of GDP are only informative when the evolution of the level of privately held financial assets from a predisturbance situation to a new long-run equilibrium follows a monotonic trajectory, we specify and consider the conditions under which these will be the case.

1 Long-run Effects of Fiscal Policy and Domestic Public Debt on the Real Levels of Exchange Rate and GDP

1.1 INTRODUCTION AND SUMMARY OF RESULTS

Some of the propositions deduced from open economy models in the Mundell–Fleming tradition have been subject to reformulations because of the implications that follow from changes in the level of foreign assets occurring as a consequence of the cumulative sum of current account imbalances induced by fiscal actions. Among these amendments are the ones investigated in this chapter, namely those relating to propositions about the effects of fiscal policy on the real levels of GDP and exchange rate, when perfect capital mobility prevails.

One of these amendments is based on an argument – originally raised by Rodriguez (1979) – which runs as follows: when an initial exchange rate appreciation is produced by a fiscal stimulus, it must be reversed in the long-run. After a sequence of capital account surplus financing the induced decline in net exports, an improvement in the trade account – and hence an exchange rate depreciation with respect to its predisturbance level – is eventually required for the current account to be balanced in the post-disturbance steady state.

This follows because of a constraint requiring the reduction in interest earnings on foreign assets, – resulting from a lower net foreign asset position of the economy – to be matched with net exports. That is, together with the initial decline of net exports induced by fiscal expansion predicted by modern versions of Mundell–Fleming models,[1] a long-run increase in the level of net exports is required to compensate for cumulative changes in interest earnings.

1

Sachs (1980), who further developed these ideas, argued that the feasibility of the proposition implied by this argument required an additional consideration. Namely, what is needed is an explicit analysis of the supply-side conditions that could make a long-run improvement in international competitiveness possible.

In this chapter we deploy an open economy model with a supply-side relationship and a demand side in the Mundell–Fleming tradition. In contrast to modern reformulations of the Mundell–Fleming model – such as the one elaborated by Frenkel and Razin (1987), that consider the total level of taxation to be autonomously determined, we explicitly state that changes in GDP and in the level of taxation are positively related.

Our main objective is to address two questions. The first of these is about the Mundell–Fleming proposition of the effects of fiscal policy when perfect capital mobility prevails. The question is, how must the robustness of this proposition be qualified when long-run changes in the level of domestic public debt are part of the analysis? That is, we are concerned with long-run effects on real exchange rate and GDP of a sequence of fiscal imbalances, and not of a balanced fiscal-budget expansion, as in the work by Branson and Buiter (1983).

The second question is: what is the role played by different assumptions about flexibility of the real levels of wages to determine the relationship between public expenditure and GDP? Unlike the work of Rodriguez and Sachs, ours fulfills the requirements of a consistent stock-flow equilibrium in the long run in order to address this latter question.

The framework presented here enables us to highlight cases of incompatibility of the structure of the model with the postulate that the authorities can consider the level of public expenditure as exogenously determined, even when variations in interest payments on government bonds are exactly matched by autonomous changes in taxation.

We show that this kind of incompatibility must be explicitly identified in order to consider a proposition suggested by Sachs (1980) in his analysis of the implications for the Mundell–Fleming model when *real* levels of wages are postulated to be rigid. He concluded that excluding the assumption of real consumer wage flexibility from the analysis leads to the result that the long-run multiplier on GDP of an exogenously determined variation in the level of public expenditure has a negative sign. In our analysis this result does not follow.

With our model we analyze fiscal effects in cases in which the real level of wages is flexible and cases in which it is not. Even in the latter cases, the levels of GDP and public expenditure are positively related.

We demonstrate that the long-run effects of a fiscal expansion that increases the level of domestic public debt can be a real exchange rate devaluation *and* a lower level of GDP, when the real level of wages is rigid.

We stress that these results do not imply a negatively signed long-run multiplier of public expenditure on GDP. We posit that they arise because a non-temporary increase in the level of public expenditure that induces a sequence of current account deficits and augments the level of domestic public debt is incompatible with the consistent specification of the long-run equilibrium of the model.

Our arguments show that, when supply-side restrictions render a higher level of production and exports impossible, a deflationary use of fiscal instruments must eventually be enforced for a steady state current account equilibrium to be achieved.

Since the level of GDP at a new steady state must be, in this case, below its predisturbance situation, the implication suggested in this chapter is that, following an initial increase in public expenditure, there must be, at some point, a reduction in the level of this variable. Moreover, we stress that this reduction in public expenditure must be larger in absolute value than the initial increase, thereby inducing the fall in GDP.

In turn, since a long-run increase in the level of net exports is required to compensate for cumulative changes in interest earnings on foreign assets, a lower level of GDP contributes to a reduction in the level of imports relative to the predisturbance equilibrium situation, partly compensating, in this way, for the lower flow of interest earnings. The remaining part of the variation in the service account of the balance of payments would correspond to the increase in net exports owing to the exchange rate depreciation.

This chapter is structured as follows. In the next section we present our model and consider the equations that constitute the demand side of the economy for the steady-state representation of the model. We append a supply-side relationship in order to highlight the role played by the assumption about the downward flexibility in the real level of wages.

We then analyze, in a third section, the conditions under which the long-run effects of an expansionary fiscal policy can be a higher level of GDP and a devaluation of the exchange rate – the conjecture originally advanced by Rodriguez (1979).

In the fourth and final section we consider how our model is modified when the assumption about a real level of wages that can be adjusted downward is substituted by another one. This is to postulate that the real level of wages is either rigid or determined by given variations in productivity.

1.2 A MUNDELL–FLEMING MODEL WITH A SUPPLY SIDE

Our analysis is based on a portfolio model for a small, open economy. Due to the nature of the problem studied, we concentrate exclusively on steady-state (long-run) effects of exogenous shocks.

1.2.1 Specification of the Model

The model is constituted by the following equations.
Stock–flow relationships:

$$e = \frac{r_0^*}{(X_q - Z_q)}l + \frac{Z_y}{(X_q - Z_q)}Y \tag{1.1}$$

$$F = F_y Y + F_N r_0^* l + F_r r \qquad F_y, F_N F_r > 0 \tag{1.2}$$

Flow relationships:

$$X = (X_q - Z_q)e - Z_y Y \qquad (X_q - Zq), Z_y > 0 \tag{1.3}$$

$$C = C_y(1 - T_y)Y + C_N r_0^* l + C_r r + C_w F$$
$$C_y, C_N, C_w > 0; C_r < 0 \tag{1.4}$$

$$YD = Y - T + (r_0 b + r b_0) + r_0^* l \tag{1.5}$$

$$T = T_y Y + T_a \qquad 0 < T_y < 0 \tag{1.6}$$

$$T_a = r_0 b + r b_0 \tag{1.7}$$

Stock relationships:

$$l = F - (b + h) \tag{1.8}$$

$$(b + h) = \lambda_0 Y + Y_0 \lambda \qquad \lambda_0 > 0 \tag{1.9}$$

$$F^d = F \tag{1.10}$$

Uncovered interest rate parity condition:

$$r = r^* \tag{1.11}$$

Supply-side relationships:

$$Y^s = Y \tag{1.12}$$

$$Y^s = \beta_1 w + \beta_2 e \qquad \beta_1, \beta_2 < 0 \tag{1.13a}$$

$$Y^s = \beta_1 (w - k) + \beta_2 e \qquad \beta_1, \beta_2 < 0 \tag{1.13b}$$

Money and goods market equilibrium condition:

$$h = H_y Y + H_r r + H_w F \qquad H_y, H_w > 0; H_r < 0 \tag{1.14}$$

$$Y = C + G + X \tag{1.15}$$

Rigid real wages assumption:

$$w = k \tag{1.16}$$

1.2.2 Description of the Model

The model represents the economy in its long-run equilibrium. This is stationary, since it abstracts from growth of GDP.

Balance of payments and private savings in steady state

Saving behavior when the economy is not in the long-run equilibrium represents an adjustment of the stock of wealth to a long-run level desired by the private sector. Non-zero savings, in turn, are linked to the current account balance and to fiscal deficits.

The long-run equilibrium is therefore identified with a situation in which assets in the system coincide with the composition and with the 'target' or long-run levels desired by the private sector.

By construction, the total expenditure of the public sector must equal its revenue in the long run. On the other hand, long-run changes in the level of public debt occur due to a sequence of fiscal deficits along the transition to the post-disturbance steady state.

In order to introduce potential long-run exchange rate adjustment linked to the effects of fiscal unbalances, the model has one property: trade balance and interest revenue on foreign assets offset each other and consequently capital flows are zero.

As in the studies of Mussa (1986) and Dornbusch and Fisher (1980) this property implies that a lower level of assets denominated in foreign currency requires an improvement of the trade balance to maintain current account equilibrium.

Net exports, X, are specified in equation (1.3) as a function of the real level of exchange rate, e, and of GDP, Y. Denoting by r_0^* the predisturbance level of the foreign interest rate and by l the variations on the levels of foreign assets, the requirement of a balanced current account in the long run is represented by equation (1.1).

Variables with the subscript '0' refer to predisturbance levels and variables without a subscript represent deviations from predisturbance values. In order to simplify the algebra we assume that at the predisturbance equilibrium the net foreign asset position of the private sector, l_0, is zero.

The variations in the level of the net stock of assets denominated in foreign currency must correspond to the discrepancy between the changes in the net stock of privately held financial assets and the sum of variations in the levels of government bonds and money. This is represented by equation (1.8). By assumption, fiscal imbalances outside the long-run equilibrium are financed only with domestic-currency-denominated assets.

Fiscal and monetary policy

Total level of taxation, T, is given by equation (1.6), where T_y is the tax rate out of income and T_a is a lump-sum tax.

In turn, the parameter λ_0 in equation (1.9) represents the predisturbance ratio of the sum of money and bonds as a share of GDP, viz:

$$\lambda_o = (b_0 + h_0)/Y_0$$

In order to consider the long-run effects of fiscal policy we rely on a number of *ad hoc* assumptions to simplify the analysis. We assume that, together with the decision to make active use of the fiscal instruments, the authorities set a target to be achieved. This is, that the long-run change in the proportion of money and government bonds in GDP has to be equal to λ.

This assumption implies relationship (1.9), where λ represents exogenously determined variations across steady states of the share of domestic-currency-denominated assets in GDP.

As explained below, we also introduce a set of assumptions that makes the velocity of money a constant in steady state. Under these assumptions the target of the economic authorities could alternatively have been restated as a share of government bonds in GDP.[2]

A rationale for this assumption could be provided on the basis of an idea suggested by Giavazzi *et al.* According to these authors, one could easily model a process whereby the government intervenes when bonds (or an appropriate ratio) hit a ceiling or floor. The ceiling or flow will then describe the stationary state (Giavazzi *et al.*, 1983, p. 4).

The achievement of this target and the balancing of fiscal accounts requires postulates of the authorities, behavior out of steady state. One of these postulates is that the level of a lump-sum tax is adjusted in order to achieve two results: the financing of interest payments on public debt and the partial closing of the gap between initial and the targeted long-run ratio on money and bonds as a share of GDP.

This assumed behavior for the economic authorities implies that once the targeted ratio is achieved, the fiscal deficit will have to be zero. In this case the lump-sum tax is given by equation (1.7). According to this equation, in the long run the government increases its flow of revenue by means of lump-sum taxes to pay for the additional interest payments. The policy rules assumed for the authorities implies that equation (1.9) will hold in the long run.

In addition, we assume that the authorities undertake actions in order to ensure that changes in the demand for money are accommodated. The money market equilibrium condition is represented by equation (1.14).

We follow this procedure in order to avoid an issue highlighted by Branson and Buiter (1983). Namely, when the nominal level of the money supply is assumed constant, the long-run level of domestic prices must change as a result of a policy action that induces a variation in one of the arguments of the money demand function.

As pointed out by Tobin and Braga de Macedo (1980), one of the channels through which fiscal policy affects the level of GDP is the effect that a variation in the exchange rate has on the money market equilibrium condition, either because foreign assets held by the private sector (including interest earnings) are specified as arguments for the demand for money – for example, Frenkel and Razin (1987) – or because of variations in the real level of the supply of money via changes in the price deflator. In our analysis we play down this channel in order to focus on the effect on the real exchange rate associated with an induced long-run deterioration of the service account when variations in the level of government bonds and imports resulting from different levels of GDP play a key role.

Due to an uncovered interest rate parity condition, long-run changes in the levels of domestic and foreign interest rate are equal to each other. This is represented by equation (1.11).

Variations in the level of GDP are equal to the changes across steady state in the levels of consumption, C, public expenditure, G, and net exports, viz equation (1.3). This is because the stock of capital is, *ex hypothesis*, constant in steady state, and hence the level of investment is zero.

Our model includes a consumption function, C, given by equation (1.4), where r represents variations in the real level of the domestic interest rate, and $r_0^* l$ represents variations in private disposable income owing to different levels of interest earnings on foreign assets.

The consumption function must be consistent with a saving function that depends on the divergence between desired and actual levels of wealth, F^d and F respectively. When these two variables are equal – as represented by relationship (1.10) – private savings are zero.

This implies, on the one hand that consumption is equal to private disposable income, YD – a variable represented by (1.5).

On the other hand, it also implies that the parameters of equation (1.2), which determines the total level of financial assets, are given by the parameters of the consumption function. That is, that the following identities hold:

$$F_y \equiv [(1 - C_y)(1 - T_y)]/C_w \, ; \qquad F_N \equiv [(1 - C_N)/C_w \, ;$$
$$F_r \equiv -(C_r/C_w)$$

Notice that substituting (1.6) and (1.7) in the definition of disposable income, (1.5), this becomes equal to consumption, once (1.2) is used to substitute for the variable F in (1.4).

Supply side

In order to contrast the results of our analysis with those presented by Sachs (1980), we follow this author in the specification of the aggregate supply relationship.

For conceptual clarity we define the level of aggregate supply, Y^s, as the (endogenously determined) level of output that profit-maximizing producers would be willing to supply for a given set of wages and relative prices, under unlimited factor supply.

In line with the non-market-clearing models for the labor market, for example, Branson and Rotemberg (1980), we postulate that employment is determined along the labor-demand function; that the real wage is above its equilibrium value and that labor is constrained in the amount of hours that employers buy.

Along with the study by Sachs (1980), we represent an aggregate supply relationship on the basis of the following postulates:

– Technology is characterized by a production function that exhibits declining marginal productivity of labor. Consistent with the assumption of profit maximization, producers hire labor until its marginal productivity is equal to the own product wage.

– The relevant real wage for workers, w, is the nominal wage deflated by the consumer price level, that is, the so-called 'real consumption wage'. The consumer price level is determined both by the producers' price level and by the price level of imports. This definition enables us to postulate that an increase in the price of imports – i.e. a devaluation – induces an increase in the price of consumer goods, even if it does not affect the price level of produced goods.

This implies that changes in the level of the real product wage for domestic producers – that is, nominal wage deflated by the level of domestically produced goods – will not necessarily coincide with variations in the level of the real (consumption) wage, w.

These postulates enable us to append to our model a relationship determining variations in the level of aggregate supply, Y^s, as a function of variations in the real levels of wages and of the real exchange rate.

In order to deduce a relationship with these characteristics, Sachs assumed a constant share of domestic goods in domestic consumption. With this assumption he expressed the consumer price level as a well-specified relationship of the producer price level and of the exchange rate. As a final step he used this relationship to re-express his aggregate supply function. A representation of this final function is given by equation (1.13a). This equation relates variations in exchange rate, real consumer wages and aggregate supply.

The negative sign for the parameter β reflects the proposition that '[f]or any real wage, an increase in the terms of trade [that is, a real appreciation of the exchange rate level] reduces the product wage, thus raising aggregate supply'.[3]

A similar proposition is presented by Branson and Rotemberg (1980), who stressed that this implication follows from postulating that employment is determined along the labor-demand function because the relevant real wage is above its equilibrium level. These two authors also suggest the way in which the analysis must be modified when a labor-supply function is added in order to have a real level of wages endogenously determined.

Sachs ignored considerations related to the stock of capital and represented, as a first step, the level of aggregate supply as a function of the nominal wage deflated by the producer price level, that is, the real product wage. Dreze and Modigliani (1981) followed a similar approach, although they were more explicit in differentiating between short- and long-run aggregate supply or 'capacity output'. The former is constrained by the existing plants and equipment. The latter is affected by depreciation or scrapping of existing plants and by investment.

Let k represent an exogenously given change in productivity. Then, as specified in equation (1.13b) when this variable is considered, an increase in productivity larger than an increase in real wages has a positive effect on aggregate supply. In turn, the particular case in which real wage rigidity exists is represented by equation (1.16).

Our steady-state equilibrium is constrained to be characterized by a zero rate of domestic inflation. It must be pointed out that imposing this constraint is tantamount to postulating that capital losses on assets denominated in domestic currency are ruled out of the steady-state solution of the model. In doing so, we are explicitly ruling out the crowding-out of private expenditure that, through this channel, could occur as a consequence of a non-zero fiscal deficit.

Our assumptions imply that at a new steady state the variations in the equilibrium level of GDP and of aggregate supply must be equal to each other, viz equation (1.12).

Model solution

The equations representing the demand side of the model can be complemented with two alternative set of relationships representing the supply side of the economy: when variations in the real level of wages are assumed to be flexible and when they are postulated to be exogenously determined.

We therefore analyze two different versions of the model: one when real wages are flexible, in which case we include (1.13a) and not (1.13b) and (1.16); the other when real wages are rigid, in which case we include (1.13b) instead of (1.13a). If, in addition, we include rigid real wage assumption as a particular case, we also include (1.16).

1.3 EFFECTIVENESS OF FISCAL POLICY IN CHANGING THE LEVEL OF GDP: THE CASE OF A DOWNWARD-FLEXIBLE REAL WAGE

In this version of the model equation (1.16) is not included and the supply function is represented by (1.13a). Hence, for a given equilibrium level of aggregate demand, Y, equation (1.12) solves for the long-run variations in the level of aggregate supply, Y^s. In turn, for given changes in levels of the real exchange rate and of

GDP, equation (1.13a) determines the long-run variations in the real level of consumer wages, w.

The steady state equilibrium is therefore determined by the equations solving for long-run deviations in the real values of the following variables: consumption, C, GDP, Y, exchange rate, e, the cumulative sum of fiscal deficit, $(b + h)$, the levels of foreign assets, l, of the net stock of privately held financial assets, F, of the stock of money, h, the level of the domestic interest rate, r, of aggregate supply, Y^s and real consumption wage, w. The variables G, λ and r_0^* are in the set of exogenously determined variables.

1.3.1 Reduced-form Solution

In order to solve for the long-run equilibrium of the system, we focus our attention on the following two equations, which constitute the reduced form of the system.

These two equations solve for the equilibrium levels of the real exchange rate, e, and of the net stock of privately held financial assets, F, for given values of public expenditure, G, of the share of domestic-currency-denominated assets in GDP, λ, and of the level of the foreign interest rate, r_0^*.

$$e = -\left[\frac{r_0^*}{(X_q - Z_q)}\right]F + \left[\frac{(Z_y + \lambda_0 r_0^*)}{(X_q - Z_q)T_y}\right]G + \left[\frac{r_0^* Y_0)}{(X_q - Z_q)}\right]\lambda \quad (1.17)$$

$$e = -\left[\frac{1}{F_N(X_q - Z_q)}\right]F + \left[\frac{(F_y + F_N Z_y)}{F_N(X_q - Z_q)T_y}\right]G + \left[\frac{F_r}{F_N(X_q - Z_q)}\right]r^*$$
$$(1.18)$$

The first relationship determines the combination of long-run equilibrium values of real exchange rate and of the stock of privately held financial assets – e and F – for which the current account is balanced.

Substituting for the level of foreign assets, l, by means of (1.8) in (1.1) and rearranging terms gives equation (1.17).

The second relationship determines the combination of long-run equilibrium levels of e and F at which the available level of the net stock of privately held financial assets is equal to the long-run level desired by the private sector.

As discussed below, it can safely be stated that as a result of the kind of fiscal expansion under consideration – with λ and G positive – the long-run level of the exchange rate depreciates.

We also determine the conditions under which both the real level of the exchange rate and of the net stock of privately held financial assets increase, as a result of a fiscal expansion that increases the level of public expenditure and the share of domestic-currency-denominated financial assets in GDP.

In order to arrive at this result, we first solve for the equilibrium levels of e and F. Substituting for F in (1.17), using (1.20), we get the exchange rate in terms of the exogenous variables:

$$e = \frac{[r_0^*(\lambda - F_y) + Z_y(1 - r_0^*F_N)]}{[(X_q - Z_q)(1 - r_0^*F_N)]T_y} G + \frac{r_0^*Y_0}{[(X_q - Z_q)(1 - r_0^*F_N)]} \lambda$$
$$- \frac{r_0^*F_r}{(X_q - Z_q)(1 - r_0^*F_N)} r^* \tag{1.19}$$

On the other hand, using (1.19) in (1.18) we can find the solution for the equilibrium level of the net stock of privately held financial assets. After rearranging, term (1.18) can be represented by:

$$F = \frac{(F_y - F_N r_0^* \lambda_0)}{(1 - r_0^*F_N)T_y} G - \frac{F_N r_0^* Y_0}{(1 - r_0^*F_N)} \lambda + \frac{F_r}{(1 - r_0^*F_N)} r^* \tag{1.20}$$

For exchange rate depreciation to occur, the following inequality must hold:

$$F_N < 1/r_0^* \tag{1.21}$$

This implies a value of less than the inverse of the foreign interest rate for the partial derivative of the long-run desired net stock of financial assets with respect to real interest revenue on non-monetary financial assets.

Since this derivative is less than unity, (1.21) holds. Hence, the coefficient of the changes in the share of domestic-currency-denominated financial assets in GDP, λ, has an unambiguously positive value.

In turn, the coefficient corresponding to the changes in the level of public expenditure is positive, provided that the following inequality holds:

$$-\{[r_0^*(\lambda_0 - F_y)]/(1 - r_0^* F_N)\} < Z_y \qquad (1.22)$$

The left-hand side of this inequality has a positive sign when the partial derivative of the long-run desired level of privately held financial assets with respect to the level of GDP, F_y, is larger than the predisturbance ratio of domestic-currency-denominated financial assets to GDP, λ_0.

When marginal and average propensities are equal to each other, the terms in brackets in the numerator on the left-hand side of this inequality can be considered to represent the negative of the partial derivative of the demand for foreign assets with respect to the level of GDP. The parameter of the right-hand side represents the propensity to import out of GDP.

With a positive variation in public expenditure, the induced level of imports due to a higher level of GDP will exercise pressure for a devaluation. The induced changes in the level of interest earnings on foreign assets will also exert pressure for a devaluation, unless the fall in the level of foreign assets due to an increase in domestic-currency-denominated assets that is, $Y_0\lambda$ – is offset by an increase in the demand for foreign assets resulting from a larger size of the portfolio that is, the effect captured by $(\lambda_0 - F_y)$.

Even if the latter effect dominates the former, their net effect would have to outweigh that of an induced increase in imports for a devaluation not to be the result of the fiscal expansion. Hence we can conclude that the variation in the real level of exchange rate is positive.

We finally determine the conditions under which both the real level of the exchange rate and of the net stock of privately held financial assets increase as a result of a fiscal expansion.

According to equation (1.20), a *ceteris paribus* increase in public expenditure increases the level of the net stock of privately held financial assets. On the other hand, the coefficient of the changes in the ratio of domestic-currency-denominated assets to GDP has a negative sign.

The positive sign is attributed to positive variations in GDP induced by a permanent change in public expenditure – that is, $(1/T_y)G$. These variations increase the level of disposable income of the private sector, and because of this more financial wealth is demanded.

The negative effect is because positive changes in domestic assets inducing a devaluation imply a lower level of assets denominated in foreign currency. In our model, this implies lower interest earnings by the private sector and therefore a lower level of disposable income.

We can conclude that the net stock of privately held financial assets increases as a result of a fiscal expansion, provided that the induced effect due to an increase in the level of public expenditure is larger in absolute terms than the reduction in interest earning on foreign assets owing to a *ceteris paribus* increase in the cumulative sum of fiscal deficits.

Formally, we can state by means of equation (1.20) that the sign of the change in the net stock of privately held financial assets depends on how large is the increase in public expenditure, G, relative to the variations in domestic-currency-denominated assets, $Y_0\lambda$, viz:

$$G/Y_0\lambda > [(r_0^*F_NT_y)/(F_y - F_Nr_0^*\lambda_0)] \qquad (1.23)$$

A fiscal expansion induces a positive variation in the long-run level of the net stock of privately held financial assets when the combination of parameters of the model, as represented by the right hand side of this inequality, represent a lower value than the increase in public expenditure relative to the variations in domestic-currency-denominated assets.

1.3.2   Long-run Multipliers of Public Expenditure on GDP

According to the Mundell–Fleming model of international macroeconomics, the following proposition for an economy with perfect capital mobility and freely floating exchange rate holds.

A change in fiscal policy – for example, an increase in government expenditure – has no effect on output, it produces an exchange rate appreciation that yields an exactly offsetting change in the trade balance, transmitting the entire disturbance abroad. The key to the result of an exchange rate appreciation lies in the effect of fiscal policy on the direction of induced capital flows.

Rodriguez (1979) and Sachs (1980) suggested that not all the propositions derived from the Mundell–Fleming model are robust, once asset dynamics through current account imbalances and longer-run changes in the level of international indebtedness and the service of that debt are considered. They criticized the proposition relating to the ineffectiveness of fiscal policy in changing the level of GDP when perfect capital mobility prevails.

Their argument has been criticized because their analysis was not based on a framework with long-run stock and flow relationships specified in a consistent manner. According to Purvis, for example, the results by Rodriguez and Sachs 'are themselves of limited interest, since the analyses on which they are based do not impose a consistent stock-flow equilibrium in the long-run' (Purvis, 1985, p. 728).[4]

With our model, it is possible to show that the implications suggested by these authors follow precisely by enforcing a consistency in the specification of the stock and flow relations of the long-run equilibrium of the model.

One of the channels through which fiscal policy affects the level of GDP is the effect that a variation in the exchange rate has on the money market equilibrium condition, This effect has been analyzed by, among others, Branson and Buiter (1983), and is not part of our study. In their model, the long-run effect of a *balanced* fiscal budget expansion is a real exchange rate appreciation.

A zero current account of the balance of payments – such as our equation (1.1) – together with the requirement for the net stock of privately held financial assets to be at its steady state level – as represented by equations (1.2) and (1.10) – imply a unitary long-run marginal propensity to spend out of private disposable income.

That is, as has already been discussed, this implication can be verified on the one hand by substituting for F in the consumption function (1.4) using (1.2). On the other hand, by substituting (1.6) and (1.7) into (1.5), we get:

$$C = (1 - T_y)Y + r_0^* l \qquad (1.24)$$

In turn, substituting (1.24) into the income–expenditure relationship (1.3), the equation determining the variations in the level of GDP can be represented by:

$$Y = (1 - T_y)Y + r_0^* l + G + (X_q - Z_q)e - Z_y Y \qquad (1.25)$$

Using equation (1.1), which states that the current account must be balanced in the long-run equilibrium, we can further simplify (1.25) to:

$$Y = (1/T_y)G \qquad (1.26)$$

The issues raised by Rodriguez (1979) and Sachs (1980) are not related to effects due to interest payments on government bonds. Because of this, we have assumed that they are taxed away by means of a corresponding increase in autonomous taxation.

With this simplification, it is highlighted that it is only when long-run changes in the level of public expenditure are *exogenously* determined to be zero, that the (endogenously determined) long-run level of GDP does not differ from its predisturbance situation.

Hence, the long-run effect of fiscal policy on GDP – that is, a permanent increase in the level of public expenditure – is positive and equal to the inverse of the tax rate.

This proposition is dependent on the way in which the supply side of the model has been specified. In this version of the model the real level of wages is postulated to be flexible, so as to allow for an increase in international competitiveness and an increase in the level of GDP.

In this model the variations in tax revenue are determined by the propensity to tax out of GDP – that is, the tax rate, T_y, is assumed to be constant – and by changes in the level of GDP. As in the case with models for closed economies with slack capacity, the level of GDP must change by the magnitude that exactly generates a variation in tax revenue equal to a permanent change in the level of public expenditure.

Modern reformulations of the Mundell–Fleming model, such as the one deployed by Frenkel and Razin (1987), consider the total level of taxation to be autonomously determined. In contrast, we explicitly state that changes in GDP and the level of taxation are positively related.

It should be pointed out that our result is deduced by assuming an accommodating monetary policy, whereas the effects of fiscal policy are conventionally analyzed assuming that the nominal level of the money supply is constant. Unlike closed economy models, in which interest rate increases as a result of fiscal policy, here it remains constant. This is because the assumption of perfect capital mobility implies that the domestic interest rate is pinned-down by the foreign interest rate.

Equation (1.26) is a long-run implication of dynamic considerations related to unbalanced current accounts and zero variations in the rate of domestic inflation across steady states. It must hold whether real wages are flexible or not. Long-run changes in the flow of public expenditure and tax revenue must not differ from each other. When real wages are rigid, another mechanism must ensure that this condition holds. This will be analyzed in Section 1.4.

1.3.3   Foreign Trade Multipliers

An alternative way of considering the determinants of the changes in the long-run level of GDP is to consider equation (1.1), which can be rearranged as:

$$y = [(X_q - Z_q)e + r_0^* l]/Z_y \qquad (1.27)$$

By means of this last equation we can state that the parameter $(1/Z_y)$ can be identified to be the Harrod multiplier for an open economy.[5]

However, instead of a shock due to an autonomous variation in aggregate demand – an exogenous change in exports in Harrod's analysis – we must consider an aggregate constituted by two induced components: the changes in net exports due to a long-run change in the real level of the exchange rate, and the variations in interest earnings of foreign assets.

A variation in the flow of interest earnings appears as a counterpart to an induced change in aggregate demand due to the following two considerations. On the one hand, it is one of the components of the long-run changes in private disposable income. On the other, the private sector has a long-run unitary propensity to consume out of its disposable income.

Hence, the term $r_0^* l$ stands for one of the induced components of the long-run changes in the level of consumption. The other component is induced through the exchange rate devaluation.

Absorption approach to the balance of payments and the long-run multiplier of public expenditure on GDP

In this subsection we consider the way in which the ideas associated with the 'absorption approach' to the balance of payments can be applied in this model.

Using equation (1.26) we substitute for Y in equation (1.24), which determines the variations in consumption. The resulting equation is:

$$Y + r_0^* l = C + G \qquad (1.28)$$

This relationship can be interpreted as stating that for an exogenously given change in the level of public expenditure, the increase in the level of consumption must be such that the following condition holds: changes in domestic absorption, $C + G$, in the long run must not differ from variations in the level of national income.

The long-run propensity to spend out of disposable income by the private sector equals one. Therefore the reason why this condition holds is because long-run changes in disposable income, YD, are given by:

$$YD = (1 - T_y)Y + r_0^* l \qquad (1.29)$$

In turn, the variations in the level of GDP are equal to $(1/T_y)G$.

On the other hand, using equations (1.1), (1.28) and (1.12) we can represent, by means of the aggregate supply relationship (1.13a), an equation determining the variation in real level of wages that is required to ensure that changes in the level of domestic absorption will be compatible with a balanced current account in the long run:

$$w = \left[\frac{(X_q - Z_q) - \beta_2(1 + Z_y)}{\beta_1(1 + Z_y)} \right] e + \left[\frac{1}{\beta_1(1 + Z_y)} \right] (C + G) \quad (1.30)$$

This equation can be interpreted as expressing the fall in the real level of wages compatible with a higher level of domestic absorption, for a given level of real exchange rate. The coefficient of both variables is unambiguously negative.

It is by means of reductions in the real level of wages that an improvement in international competitiveness is possible, thereby allowing, by means of a devaluation, for a higher level in net exports. Since an increase in the level of exports above the requirements to compensate for higher interest payments on foreign assets implies, via a multiplier effect, an increase in the level of GDP larger than the variations in net exports, part of the increase in output is absorbed domestically.

In this model the long-run level of GDP increases because, *ex-hypothesis*:

- Employment is determined along the labor-demand function.
- Technology is characterized by declining marginal productivity of labor, and employers hire labor until its marginal productivity is equal to the own product wage.
- At a predisturbance equilibrium situation, labor was constrained by the amount of hours that employers were hiring.
- The real consumer wage is an endogenously determined variable. To state that downward movements in this variable allow for a higher level of production is tantamount to a further postulate, namely that a negative relationship exist between producers' real wages and the real level of the exchange rate.

1.4   EFFECTIVENESS OF FISCAL POLICY TO CHANGE THE LEVEL OF GDP: THE CASE OF REAL WAGE RIGIDITY

In the version of the model analyzed in previous sections the variation in the long-run level of real wages, w, was endogenously determined and the change in the level of public expenditure, G, was included among the set of exogenously determined variables.

In this section we consider how our model is modified when the assumption about a real level of wages that can be adjusted downward is substituted by another one. This alternative assumption postulates that the real level of wages is either rigid, as in equation (1.16), or, more generally, determined by an exogenously determined variation in productivity given by k and in real wages, w, can both be different from zero, but not necessarily equal to each other, as in equation (1.13b).

The analysis of this case will enable us to investigate how the incorporation of the assumption of rigid real wages affects the Mundell–Fleming proposition relating to the ineffectiveness of fiscal policy in changing the level of GDP.

In order to consider the case of rigid real consumption wages, we must include an additional equation in the model analyzed in the previous section, thereby representing explicitly the postulate that the real level of wages can only change from one steady state to another by a given value equal to k. This additional equation is (1.16).

In this extended version of the model, equation (1.16) solves for the long-run variation in the real level of wages which, *ex-hypothesis*, is determined to be equal to a constant k. Consequently, for a given change in the real level of the exchange rate, equations (1.13b) and (1.12) solve, respectively, for the long-run variations in the level of aggregate supply, Y^s, and for the equilibrium variations in the level of GDP, Y.

The inclusion of an equation constraining variations in the real level of wages in a way that is not the result of the interaction of the variables of the system, is tantamount to having one endogenously determined variable less than those that constituted the version of the model analyzed in the previous section. Therefore, for the solution of the extended version of the model, it is required that one of the variables previously identified as exogenous be considered endogenously determined.[6]

It is illustrative to select the variations in the level of public expenditure as the variable that becomes endogenously determined when variations in real wages are not endogenously determined. Hence equation (1.16) determines that the variations in the real level of wages must be equal to a constant k. In turn, equations (1.4), (1.11), (1.12) and (1.13b) solve for the variables e, F, l, C, Y, r, h, $(b + h)$, Y^s and G, for given values of λ and of the variables related to the foreign sector.

1.4.1 Equilibrium Solution

In order to find the equilibrium solution of the variables in our model we follow the same procedure as in the previous sections. We concentrate on a two-equation, reduced-form model. One equation solves for the long-run variations in the level of exchange rate – equation (1.1) – and the other solving for the long-run variations in the real levels of the net stock of privately held financial assets – equation (1.2).

The reduced-form of these equations will enable us to identify two schedules that can be represented diagrammatically in order to illustrate the determinants of the long-run variations in the equilibrium level of the exchange rate (Figure 1.1).

Using equation (1.8), we can substitute for the variations in foreign assets, l, in equation (1.1), which is the requirement of a balanced current account. In turn, substituting in this equation for Y by means of (1.13b), (1.12), (1.16) and rearranging terms, we deduce one of our relationships:

$$
\begin{aligned}
e = & -\left[\frac{r_0^*}{[(X_q - Z_q) - (Z_y + r_0^*\lambda_0)\beta_2]}\right]F \\
& +\left[\frac{r_0^* Y_0}{[(X_q - Z_q) - (Z_y + r_0^*\lambda_0)\beta_2]}\right]\lambda \\
& +\left[\frac{(Z_y + r_0^*\lambda_0)\beta_1}{[(X_q - Z_q) - (Z_y + r_0^*\lambda_0)\beta_2]}\right](w - k) \quad (EE \text{ schedule})
\end{aligned}
$$

$$(1.31)$$

In turn, the second equation determines the combinations of e and F for which available level of privately held financial assets is equal to the level desired by the private sector. By means of equation (1.2), (1.13a), (1.12) it can be deduced that:

$$
\begin{aligned}
e = & \left[\frac{(1 - F_N r_0^*)}{(F_y - F_N r_0^*\lambda_0)\beta_2}\right]F + \left[\frac{F_N r_0^* Y_0}{(F_y - F_N r_0^*\lambda_0)\beta_2}\right]\lambda \\
& -\left(\frac{\beta_1}{\beta_2}\right)(w - k) - \left[\frac{F_r}{(F_y - F_N r_0^*\lambda_0)\beta_2}\right]r^* \quad (FF \text{ schedule})
\end{aligned}
$$

$$(1.32)$$

Both schedules have a negative slope in the e, F space, as illustrated in Figure 1.1. With a positive value of λ – that is, when the share of domestic assets in the system increases as a result of a sequence of fiscal deficits – the FF schedule shifts to the left whereas the EE schedule shifts to the right.

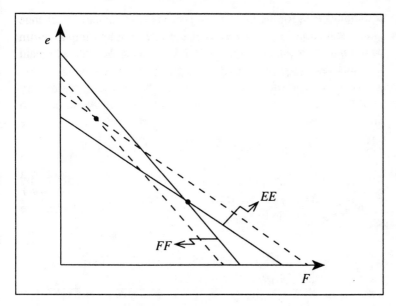

Figure 1.1   Long-run effects on the real exchange rate and on private financial
wealth of a change in domestic public debt

When the slope of the *FF* schedule is larger in absolute value than
the slope of the *EE* schedule, we can state that an increase in
cumulative sum of fiscal deficits – that is, a positive λ – induces a
devaluation.

In order for the slope of the *FF* schedule to have a larger value
in absolute value than the slope of the *EE* schedule, the following
condition must hold:

$$[(X_q - Z_q) - (Z_y + r_0^* \lambda_0)\beta_2] > (F_y - F_N r_0^* \lambda_0)\beta_2 r^*$$

Rearranging terms this inequality becomes:

$$(X_q - Z_q) + \beta_2[(F_y r_0^* - Z_y - r_o^*)^* \lambda_0 + Z_y F_N r_0^*] > 0$$

the parameter β_2 is negative, and $(X_q - Z_q)$ positive, a sufficient
but not necessary condition for this inequality to hold is:

$$[(F_y - \lambda_0)/(1 - F_N r_0^*)] < Z_y/r_0^* \qquad (1.33)$$

This condition will, in general, be fulfilled, unless the parameter representing the propensity to import out of income, Z_y, is very small. Notice that λ_0 tends to be closer to F_y the less important the initial level of foreign assets are in private portfolio, when average and marginal propensities of the total demand for assets do not differ from each other.

1.4.2   Effects on the Level of Exchange Rate

The long-run solution for the variations in the real level of the exchange rate can be deduced by substituting for F using (1.32) into equation (1.31) to get:

$$
e = \frac{(r_0^* Y_0)}{\beta_2[r_0^*(F_y - \lambda_0) - Z_y(1 - F_N r_0^*)] + (X_q - Z_q)(1 - F_N r_0^*)} \lambda
$$
$$
- \frac{\beta_1[r_0^*(F_y - \lambda_0) - Z_y(1 - F_N r_0^*)]}{\beta_2[r_0^*(F_y - \lambda_0) - Z_y(1 - F_N r_0^*)] + (X_q - Z_q)(1 - F_N r_0^*)} (w - k)
$$
$$
- \frac{r_0^* F_r}{\beta_2[r_0^*(F_y - \lambda_0) - Z_y(1 - F_N r_0^*)] + (X_q - Z_q)(1 - F_N r^*)} r^* \quad (1.34)
$$

The long-run effects of exogenous changes in the real level of exchange rate are represented by the following:

$$
e/\lambda > 0
$$
$$
e/(w - k) < 0
$$
$$
e/r^* < 0
$$

As shown in Figure 1.1, when condition (1.33) holds, a permanent increase in the cumulative sum of fiscal deficits induces a long-run exchange-rate depreciation and a fall in the real level of the net stock of privately held financial assets.

In turn, when an increase in productivity is larger than an increase in the real level of wages, a higher level of net exports can be produced. This implies that, for same level of interest payments on foreign assets, a real exchange rate depreciation follows.

Effects of an increase in the level of foreign interest rate

Why does a *ceteris paribus* permanent increase in the level of the foreign interest rate produce an exchange rate appreciation? This result contrasts with the one that would have been obtained not only with the early static versions of the Mundell–Fleming model, but also with its extended version with rational expectations, such as the one developed by Dornbusch (1976).

As explained by Kouri (1983), these frameworks do not have an adequate specification of an intertemporal balance of payments constraint. Because of this, they misspecify the long-run effects of a permanent increase in the world interest rate.

We consider the argument advanced by this author to clarify the existing relationship between an adequate specification of an intertemporal balance of payments constraint and specification of the function representing the long-run desired level of the net stock of privately held financial assets.

To understand the requirements for the long-run specification we consider first the short-run effects in the Dornbusch model. On impact, a permanent increase in the world interest rate induces a shift away from domestic into foreign assets and as a consequence the currency depreciates. This, in turn implies an improvement in the trade balance, provided that the Marshall–Lerner conditions hold. In turn, a higher real level of the interest rate induces a contractionary effect on domestic aggregate demand. In order to maintain full employment equilibrium – when this is assumed – this effect requires an increase in net exports to compensate for the fall in domestic demand.

However, unless the implications that follow from an intertemporal balance of payments constraint are adequately specified, the model will imply a permanently depreciated exchange rate level and a current account permanently in surplus.

Kouri clarifies this issue as follows:

> Consider Dornbusch's full employment version of the Mundell–Fleming model. The model implies that in response to an increase in the world interest rate the current account will be *permanently* in surplus. Clearly, this cannot be a sustainable equilibrium, but rather reflects a misspecification of the model. The misspecification that is responsible for this conclusion is the neglect of the intertemporal budget constraint, or, what comes to the same, of the effects of interest earnings (payments) on domestic absorption. (Kouri, 1983, p. 79)

Some lines later he referred to the mechanism that is not captured by the Dornbusch model:

> As long as the current account is in surplus (deficit), domestic wealth increases (decreases) and thus domestic consumption also increases (decreases). ... In the stationary equilibrium the current account is equal to zero, and the trade account surplus (deficit) is equal to net foreign interest income.
>
> ... Consider now the effect of an increase in the foreign interest rate once the requirement of long-run portfolio balance is recognized. Assume initially that full employment prevails both in the short run and in the long-run. In the short run increase in the foreign rate causes an outflow of capital, a deterioration of the terms of trade and an increase in the domestic price level. Over time the stock of foreign assets increases and causes an improvement in the terms of trade. In the new long-run equilibrium, the stock of foreign assets is higher, and the interest account surplus is greater than in the initial equilibrium. Therefore, the long-run effect of an increase in the foreign interest rate on the domestic terms of trade is *favorable*. (Kouri, 1983, pp. 78–9)

In order to avoid the type of misspecification pointed out by Kouri, two issues should not be neglected in our model. On the one hand, problems associated with flow variables are considered within a framework in which adjustment to stock equilibrium determine the intrinsic dynamics of the model. On the other hand, the consistency of the stock and flow relationships is such that the specification of the private expenditure function is inextricably linked – by means of its partial derivatives – to the specification of the function corresponding to the long-run desired level of privately held financial assets.

Hence, in our model we have the result that, under a flexible exchange rate regime with perfect capital mobility, a permanent increase in the world interest rate causes an exchange rate appreciation. This is by virtue of a mechanism that leads to a new long-run equilibrium with a balanced current account. This mechanism induces a long-run *decrease* in net exports to match for the variations in interest earnings on foreign assets accumulated during the transition to a new long-run equilibrium.

1.4.3 Effects on the Level of GDP

Our results are useful to highlight the following implications for changes in the level of GDP.

A sequence of fiscal deficits resulting from an initial increase in public expenditure implies a higher level of assets denominated in domestic currency. This kind of fiscal expansion will also induce a series of current account deficits and, as a result, the level of foreign assets held by domestic residents will be lower at a new steady state.

As in the case previously analyzed, a long-run increase in net exports is required to match a fall in interest earnings on foreign assets. This requires a depreciation of the real level of the exchange rate.

Consider now the case in which the real level of wages cannot fall relative to productivity changes. This will be the case in which w equals k, in equation (1.16). It is not possible to induce higher levels of GDP while simultaneously fulfilling the requirement that the current account be balanced in the long run.

Because of the long-run depreciation of the exchange rate, net exports increase. However the increase due to this effect is not sufficient to match for the lower level of interest earnings. Therefore a reduction in the level of imports must be induced via a lower level of GDP.

This lower level of GDP will also correspond to the level of aggregate supply that domestic producers are willing to produce at the new long-run level of real exchange rate. Because of the postulate of constant level of consumer real wages, a higher level of the exchange rate implies a higher level of the own product wage for domestic producers. In turn, due to the assumed decreasing marginal productivity of labor, the aggregate supply – derived on the basis of a profit-maximizing criterion – will be lower.

Hence, with a higher level of domestic currency denominated assets in the system because of a cumulative sum of fiscal deficits, we have the following implication for the long-run equilibrium of the model.

The initial movement in the level of public expenditure must be reversed to a level *below* its predisturbance situation. This U-turn in the movement in the level of public expenditure is required in order to ensure that the long-run balance of payments constraint is ensured.

It is for these reasons that the long-run variation in the level of public expenditure must be classified as an endogenously determined variable in a model with the following characteristics: an intertemporal balance of payments constraint, rigidity in the real level of wages and a domestic rate of inflation constrained to be the same in the two steady states under comparison.

The structure of the model is such that a long-run depreciation of the real exchange rate is a sufficient condition for the net stock of privately held financial assets, GDP, foreign assets, private consumption and public expenditure to be below their predisturbance levels as a result of an increase in the cumulative sum of fiscal deficits.

We wish to stress the following implication. When, as a consequence of the initial sequence of fiscal deficits, a long-run depreciation of the real exchange rate is induced, the equilibrium level of GDP at a new steady state will be below its predisturbance level.

This can immediately be deduced by means of equations (1.12) and (1.16), which allows us to represent equation (1.13a) by:

$$Y = \beta_2 e \qquad\qquad (1.35)$$

This negative relationship between variations in the level of GDP and of the real exchange rate when real wages are rigid led Sachs (1980) to suggest that the Mundell–Fleming proposition relating to the ineffectiveness of public expenditure to affect the level of GDP must be qualified in the case of rigidity in the real level of wages. According to this author, the long-run effect of a permanent variation in the level of public expenditure is, under these kinds of circumstance, a negative variation in the real level of GDP.

He presented this argument based on a model that has been criticized for not having an adequate specification in its stock and flow relationships. Within the framework of these characteristics, he deduced that the relationship between long-run variations in public expenditure and GDP was determined by a combination of parameters of the model. He showed that the magnitude of this combination of parameters had a positive sign in the case of rigid money wages and a negative one in the case of a rigid level of real wages.

Based on this result he concluded that whereas the long-run multiplier of public expenditure on GDP is positive in the case of rigid money wages, it has a *negative* value when the real level of wages is rigid.

Our procedure has the analytical advantage of highlighting, in a straightforward manner, that the relationship between the long-run changes in public expenditure and GDP is always positive and is determined by a single parameter – the inverse of the propensity to tax out of GDP. We have demonstrated that, when stocks and flows are consistently specified, this has to be the case whether real wages are flexible or not.

By stressing the requirement for a consistent stock-flow equilibrium in the long run we can highlight that an interpretation of a permanent increase in the level of public expenditure having a negative effect on the level of GDP is incompatible with the conclusions deduced within our model.

As has been previously indicated, in the circumstances under consideration the long-run variations in the level of GDP are negative. Although public expenditure initially increases, it must eventually not only be returned to its previous level, but also decreased somewhat. It is by means of a readjustment of this kind that the long-run level of aggregate demand decreases from its predisturbance situation.

Due to this required reversal in the direction of movements in the level of public expenditure, the long-run changes in this variable become endogenously determined as a way to ensure that the current account is balanced in the long run. The required variation in the level of public expenditure can be deduced by substituting (1.13b) into equation (1.26) and rearranging the terms, viz:

$$G = T_y \beta_2 e$$

Hence, if the result of an initial sequence of fiscal deficits is a long-run depreciation in the level of the exchange rate, a permanent reduction in the level of public expenditure is required.

This is the mechanism that ensures a long-run equilibrium in the goods market in a situation in which the authorities have to fulfil an intertemporal balance of payments constraint when real wages are rigid, and the cumulative sum of fiscal deficits was initially increased by a fiscal expansion.

Our analysis has been based on a model whose long run is characterized by a size and composition of the private sector portfolio corresponding to their long-run desired levels. This kind of model has the property of ensuring that issues relating to flow markets are considered within a framework in which stock disequilibria determine the intrinsic dynamics of the model.

1.5   CONCLUDING COMMENTS

Because expectations bring forward policy dilemmas to the present, the issues raised in this chapter should not be dismissed as longer-run concerns. The analysis presented here can be considered to complement models in which the inclusion of an aggregate supply is not disregarded, and expectations of movements in the real level of the exchange rate are assumed to be forward-looking, such as in the work by Deveroux and Purvis (1990) and Kouri (1979).

In the next chapter we analyze the dynamics of the real exchange rate when expectations about exchange rate movements are forward-looking and the level of domestic public changes. Our analysis will enable us to gain insight into the functioning and required extensions of the modern version of a stock-flow model within the Mundell–Fleming tradition.

The dynamic specification of the model presented in the next chapter has an interesting property: in contrast with the studies of other authors, in our framework the size of the fiscal deficit along the trajectory to a new long-run equilibrium is not exogenously specified. With this property we allow fiscal imbalances to change the level of domestic public indebtedness and consider its implications for exchange rate dynamics.

2 The Dynamics of Real Exchange Rate and Financial Assets of Contractionary Fiscal Policies cum Private Dissavings

2.1 INTRODUCTION AND SUMMARY OF RESULTS

In analyses of the last few years of developments concerning the balance of payments in countries such as the UK, Australia and Mexico, a commonly found claim is that current account deficits, when associated with private sector dissavings, should not be a reason for concern. One of the arguments behind this claim is that unlike public sector dissavings – that is, fiscal deficits – those corresponding to the private sector should be self-correcting in the long run. The reasoning is that agents of the private sector are not going to ignore their ex-ante intertemporal budget constraint. This implies that they will eventually want to bring spending into line with their underlying asset and debt positions.

Claims along these lines are further substantiated by pointing out that in some instances – for example, Denmark, Ireland and Mexico – private dissavings are inducing current account deficits, even though they occur simultaneously with reductions in public sector deficits. These latter reductions, on their own, would lead to a current account surplus. An explanation of a phenomenon in which private sector dissavings more than compensate for public sector savings is the effect that fiscal policy has on the perceptions the private sector has about the medium- and long-term developments in the economy. That is, since fiscal contractions are considered by the private sector to be sustainable, they are perceived to lead to long-run reductions in public indebtedness (see Giavazzi and Pagano, 1990, Hellwig and Neumann, 1987, and Calderón, 1994).

In this chapter we deploy a model for understanding the behavior of an open economy with an initial phase of its dynamic trajectory characterized by reductions in fiscal deficits accompanied by more-than-compensating reductions in private surplus, thereby exhibiting privately financed current account deficits and an appreciated exchange rate level. In addition to the consistent specification of the stock-flow dynamics, our framework incorporates expected movements in the real level of the exchange rate. These are assumed to be rational, in the sense of being self-fulfilling, because an assumption is made of perfect foresight by private agents.

This model – which follows the modern version of the Mundell–Fleming approach – enables us to consider the evolution of the real levels of the exchange rate, interest rates, and of the level and composition of private sector wealth in an open economy exhibiting these peculiarities.

The private sector in our model can hold money as well as domestic and foreign-currency-denominated non-monetary financial assets. In turn, its savings behavior is interpreted as an adjustment of the stock of wealth to a long-run level desired by this sector. Non-zero savings by the private sector are linked to fiscal and current-account balances.

In the model, the long-run equilibrium refers to a situation in which trade balance and interest revenue on foreign assets offset each other, and consequently capital flows are zero. This implies, by construction, that its steady state has two properties. First, as in the papers by Dornbusch and Fischer (1980) and Krugman (1988), the levels of real exchange rate and of net holdings of foreign assets by the private sector are inversely related across steady states. Second, variations in the level of domestic public debt are related to changes in the real level of the exchange rate: as in the work by Sachs and Wyplosz (1984), we allow fiscal imbalances to change the level of domestic public indebtedness and consider its implications for exchange rate dynamics.

Due to these peculiarities of the model, we have, at the outset, the following two implications embedded in our analysis. On the one hand, stating that a long-run decrease in the real level of the cumulated sum of the domestically-financed fiscal deficits – that is, the level of domestic public indebtedness – is perceived as feasible by the private sector, is tantamount to stating that a long-run real exchange rate appreciation is expected to take place. On the other hand, if *ex-hypothesis* short-run private sector dissavings more than compensate for public sector savings, then an initial exchange rate appreciation must occur for the implied current account deficit to be registered.

These two implications, in turn, generate the following question. How can both a short- and long-run real exchange rate appreciation be possible, given the constraint requiring that long-run variations in interest earnings on foreign assets, resulting from a different net foreign asset position of the economy, be matched with net exports at a post-disturbance steady state?

The answer to this question, to be explored in this chapter, is that the exchange rate must follow a dynamic trajectory that enables a sequence of current account deficits to be more than compensated by a sequence of current account surpluses.

One possibility arises if there are no productivity gains in the tradable sector. In this case the trajectory of the exchange rate must have a cyclical or non-monotonic convergence path to its new long-run equilibrium. This is so because an initial sequence of exchange rate appreciation must be followed by a temporary sequence of an exchange rate depreciated with respect to the predisturbance level.

Whenever the real exchange rate is below its predisturbance level the current account is in deficit, and consequently a reduction in the level of foreign assets held by the private sector takes place. A long-run exchange rate appreciation is associated with an increase in the level of foreign assets. Therefore, there must be an eventual reversal of the movement in the level of foreign assets during the transition to the long run. For these reversals to occur, the convergence path of the real exchange rate must be non-monotonic, thereby enabling changes in the level of foreign assets owing to a sequence of current account surplus to be larger than the absolute value of the change in assets owing to current account deficits.

A further possibility, which will not be explored in this study, is the following: a non-monotonic behavior of the exchange rate –

that is, a depreciation alternating with an appreciation – would not be required if the model could adequately incorporate productivity gains. This would enable a more competitive export sector, and hence a current account surplus, without requiring an exchange rate depreciation.

Most existing analytical models with forward-looking expectations of exchange rate behavior share the limitations of our model in addressing the second answer.[1] In addition, due to the reduced size of their dynamic system, they are ill-equipped to consider the first answer as well, and to explicitly consider the evolution of the *size* of the private sector financial portfolio.

It is a common procedure to rely on a dynamic system with less than three dynamic equations. This procedure rules out, by construction, a non-monotonic behavior of the exchange rate. This follows because of the forward-looking assumption about exchange rate movements. Due to this assumption, the models must exhibit saddle-point characteristics, that is, associated with a non-predetermined or 'jump' variable there must be one unstable root in the dynamic system. The influence of this root is neutralized – by means of a transversality condition – thereby constraining the system to lie on the stable manifold.[2]

Our study analyses the non-monotonic case in an analytically tractable model, and in the process enables us to gain insight into the functioning and required extensions of the modern version of a stock-flow model within the Mundell–Fleming tradition.[3]

The remaining part of this chapter is divided into two sections.

In Section 2.2 we present the model, discuss its dynamic structure and analyze the characteristics of the long-run equilibrium of the model. On the basis of these characteristics we analyze the way in which a change in domestic public indebtedness is related to the real levels of the exchange rate and the net stock of privately held financial assets.

In Section 2.3 we consider the response that shocks to the system would have on the short-run or impact levels of exchange and interest rates. We discuss the characteristics of the dynamic trajectory to the new steady state and explain why a non-monotonic convergence path would be registered with the problem addressed in this chapter.

We finally specify and interpret the conditions under which the long-run equilibrium of the model has the saddle-point properties required owing to the forward-looking nature of expectations about exchange rate movements.

2.2   A DYNAMIC MODEL OF THE REAL EXCHANGE RATE

Our analysis is based on a portfolio model for a small, open economy represented by the following fifteen equations, plus one constraint on the value of Ω in equation (2.15), to be described below in our discussion about the composition of fiscal deficit financed with money. The consistency between stock-flow relationships is stressed and forward-looking expectations about exchange rate movements is assumed. All variables represent deviations from predisturbance situations, except those with subscript '$_0$' which denote predisturbance levels.

2.2.1   Specification of the Model

Expectational Variables and Flow Relationships:

$$e_t^e = (de/dt)(1/e_t) \tag{2.1}$$

$$Y_t = C_t + G_t + X_t - Z_t \tag{2.2}$$

$$X_t - Z_t = (X_q - Z_q)e_t + Z_y Y_t$$
$$(X_q - Z_q) > 0; Z_y < 0 \tag{2.3}$$

$$C_t = C_y Y_t - C_T T_t + C_N N_t + C_v[l_0(de/dt)(1/e_t)]$$
$$+ C_r r_t + C_w F_t + C_t^a$$
$$C_y = C_T = C_N > 0; C_v, C_w > 0; C_r \le 0 \tag{2.4}$$

$$N_t = r_0 b_t + B_0 r_t + r_0^*(l_t + l_0 e_t) \tag{2.5}$$

$$G_t = -(C_t + X_t - Z_t) \tag{2.6}$$

$$T_t = r_0 b_t + r_t b_0 \tag{2.7}$$

Financial Markets:

$$F_t = h_t + b_t + (l_t + l_0 e_t) \tag{2.8}$$

$$H_y Y_t + H_t r_t + H_w F_t = h_t \qquad H_y, H_w > 0; H_r < 0 \qquad (2.9)$$

$$\rho_t = \rho_1 (l_t + l_0 e_t) + \rho_2 F_t - \rho_2 h_t$$
$$\rho_1 < 0; \rho_2 > 0; -\rho_1 > \rho_2 \qquad (2.10)$$

$$r_t = r_t^* + \rho_t + e_t^e \qquad (2.11)$$

Dynamic Equations:

$$(dl/dt) = (X_q - Z_q)e_t + r_0^* l_t + l[r_0^* e_t + (de/dt)(1/e_t)] \quad (2.12)$$

$$(dF/dt) = (1 - C_N)r_0^*(l_t + l_0 e_t) + [(1 - c_v)l_0 - C_r]$$
$$(de/d_t)(1/e) - C_r(r_t^* + \rho_t) - C_w F_t - C_t^a \qquad (2.13)$$

$$(de/dt)(1/e) = -\rho_1 l_t - [\rho_2 + (H_w/H_r)]F_t - l_0 \rho_1 e_t$$
$$+ [(1/H_r) + \rho_2]h_t \qquad (2.14)$$

$$(dh/dt) = \Omega(G_t + r_0 b_t + r b_0 - T_t) \qquad (2.15)$$

Expectational variables and flow relationships

Expected movements in the real level of the exchange rate, e^e, are assumed to be rational, in the sense of being self-fulfilling, because of the assumption of perfect foresight. This is represented by equation (2.1). The term on the right-hand side of this equation stands for the actual rate of change in the real level of the exchange rate, represented by the variable e.

Equation (2.2) is the conventional goods market equilibrium condition, which states that in deviations from the predisturbance situation the real level of GDP, Y, must be equal to the sum of desired private expenditure, C, public expenditure, G, and net exports, $X - Z$. In turn, the net level of exports, as represented by equation (2.3), is specified as a function of the real level of domestic GDP and of the real level of the exchange rate.

By means of equation (2.4) we postulate a linearised private expenditure function depending on the levels of disposable income and assume that the propensity to consume out of the four components of private disposable income – GDP, taxes, T, interest earnings, N, and capital gains – do not differ from each other. The real levels of financial wealth, F, and of the domestic interest rate, r, are also among its determinants. We have added the term C^a – this allows us to represent non-permanent autonomous changes in the level of private expenditure with respect to its predisturbance level.

The variable N, defined as the real level of interest revenue on non-monetary financial assets, which are either government bonds, b, or foreign assets, l, is represented by equation (2.5). In turn, r_0^*, which represents the predisturbance real level of the foreign interest rate, is assumed to be fixed. The financial assets are specified in real terms by deflating their nominal value (expressed in domestic currency) by the producer's price index. As explained below, domestic price changes are assumed away, hence capital gains and losses due to asset price changes are only those represented by $l_0(de/dt)/e$.

Our main concern is the dynamic adjustment path of an open economy with an initial phase of its trajectory characterized by a public sector having a surplus accompanied by a more than compensating reduction in private surplus, thereby exhibiting privately financed current account deficits. We are particularly concerned with capturing the financial effects of fiscal policy when changes in the level of domestic-currency government bonds are explicitly considered, but not in a predetermined way.

In order to simplify the dynamics of a system capable of capturing these effects, we concentrate on the case in which the economic authorities, in the event of a variation in private expenditure, engage in an active use of public expenditure to ensure that the real level of aggregate demand remains constant. This assumption is stated by equation (2.6). It implies that the variable Y, which represents deviations of GDP from their predisturbance levels, is zero because it is not the level but the composition of aggregate demand that changes. It also implies that pressures on the domestic price level due to excess demand for goods are ruled out by assumption.

Moreover this simplification allows for a dynamic specification with a desired property: in contrast with the policy rule postulated by other authors,[4] ours implies that the size of the fiscal deficit along the trajectory to a new long-run equilibrium is not exogenously specified.

On the other hand, since we are not interested in the potential source of instability associated with the *domestic* debt service component, we assume that the government increases its revenue flow by means of lump-sum taxes to pay for the additional interest payments. That is, T is a lump-sum tax determined according to equation (2.7).

Our set of assumptions is useful to simplify the algebra. It ensures that changes in private disposable income can be due only to two effects. The first is changes in the real flow of interest earnings on assets denominated in foreign currency, and the other is variations in the real level of these assets due to movements in the real exchange rate.

To analyze the long-run and dynamic properties of the model, we consider the case of a *temporary* change in the autonomously determined component of private expenditure, viz. a non-permanent positive value of C^a. This component is determined at a value of zero except for a temporary period, at the initial phase of a dynamic trajectory, in which it acquires a positive value. Notice that according to equation (2.6), this change in private expenditure takes place simultaneously with a fiscal surplus, by means of which public debt is withdrawn. When the autonomous component C^a returns to its initial value of zero, the fiscal budget and the current account remain unbalanced until the intrinsic dynamics of the system lead the economy to a new long-run equilibrium – provided that the required saddle-point properties are fulfilled.

Financial markets

In order to consider current account imbalances financed exclusively by the private sector, we assume that the public sector neither finances its deficit with foreign indebtedness nor holds foreign assets. If it is exogenously determined, foreign financing to the public sector can easily be incorporated. Its explicit exclusion is analytically advantageous. It enables us to represent the discrepancy between the variation in the level of the net stock of assets to be held by the private sector and the change in the level of foreign assets as the counterpart to the financing of the fiscal deficit.

Equation (2.8), which states that financial wealth is equal to the sum of its components – namely money, h, bonds and foreign-currency denominated assets – holds at any point in time. The demand for money is represented as a function of GDP,[5] of the domestic interest rate and of the real level of wealth. The money market equilibrium condition is therefore given by (2.9). In our analysis, two of the arguments of the demand for money change across steady states: the real levels of private sector wealth and of the domestic interest rate.

Risk-premium is represented in (2.10) by ρ. This equation is deduced from a portfolio-balanced model specification following Sachs and Wyplosz (1984). The procedure is based on a linearization of the equations of a balanced portfolio model, obtaining the risk premium as a function of the relative levels of the foreign- and domestic-currency-denominated non-monetary assets. F and h appear in equation (2.10) instead of b by means of equation (2.8).

The long-run levels of the domestic interest rate change when the levels of foreign interest rate and/or the risk-premium change. During the transition to a new long-run equilibrium, the level of domestic interest rate is also determined by the expectations of exchange rate movements in such a way as to fulfill the covered interest rate parity condition, as specified by equation (2.11).

Dynamic equations

Variations in the level of foreign assets at a point in time, as represented by equation (2.12), are induced either by an unbalanced current account or by the revaluation of existing assets denominated in foreign currency.

We have explicitly incorporated a number of assumptions in order to identify variations in private disposable income with only two of its components, namely interest earnings on foreign assets and capital gains and losses due to exchange rate movements. Subtracting from the flow of private disposable income the flow of private expenditure, we get an aggregate that corresponds to the change, at a given point in time, of the demand for the net stock of privately held financial assets, dF/dt. This is represented by equation (2.13).

Notice that, the following relationships holds – and can be deduced from equations (2.12), (2.13), (2.3), (2.4) and (2.6):

$$(dF/dt) - [(dl/dt) + l_0(de/dt)(1/e_0)]$$
$$= G_t + r_0 b_t + b_0 r_t - T_t \tag{2.16}$$

This equation indicates that public sector deficits are financed by domestic-currency-denominated bonds or by money.

In order to deduce the differential equation that specifies how changes in the exchange rate are determined, we use the money market equilibrium condition (2.9) together with the covered interest rate parity condition (2.11). *Ex hypothesis,* these two equations hold at any point in time along the transition between an initial point after a shock occurred and a new long-run equilibrium. Using equation (2.1) to substitute for e^e in equation (2.11) and solving for r with the resulting equation, we can restate (2.9) by (2.14).

As will be discussed below, in this model the long-run money market equilibrium must be consistent with a level of interest rate determined by the interest rate parity condition represented by (2.11), when expected movements of the exchange rate are zero. For this requirement to be fulfilled, the assumed behavior of the monetary authorities must accordingly be modelled, given that the domestic price level cannot take the role of the adjusting variable. We therefore assume a behavior for the monetary authorities that ensures that *long-run* changes in the demand for money are accommodated. That is, the long deviations of the supply of money with respect to a predisturbance level become one of the variables determined endogenously by the model. How can this property be incorporated into our model?

To answer this question we first notice that, along the transition to a new long-run equilibrium, a fiscal deficit is financed with money and government bonds. Assuming, as in equation (2.15), that the public sector finances a share, Ω, of its fiscal deficit with money, enables us to have the required accommodating monetary policy in the long run. It will be shown that this is so, provided that this share is equal to the proportion of total change in money with respect to the cumulative sum of fiscal deficits resulting in the long run. That is, when it is equal in the long run to the coefficient $h/(h+b)$, which results in a magnitude determined by the parameters of the model.

It is worth pointing out that this assumption does *not* preclude money market disequilibria, whether during the transition to a new long-run equilibrium or at the moment that a shock to the system occurs. A change in the level of the supply of money does not necessarily coincide with a variation in the demand for money at the point in time at which the change in supply occurs. In addition, this assumption has the property of allowing us to consider, within an analytically tractable framework, those cases in which a constant price deflator of the money supply is consistent with a money market equilibrium condition.[6]

2.2.2 Steady-State Representation

$$r = r^* + \rho_1(l + l_0 e) + \rho_2 F - \rho_2 h \tag{2.17}$$

$$l = F - (h + b) - l_0 e \tag{2.18}$$

$$\begin{aligned} h =& [H_r/(1 + \rho_2 H_r)] + \rho_1(l + l_0 e) \\ &+ [H_r/(1 + \rho_2 H_r)][\rho_2 + (H_w/H_r)]F \\ &+ [H_r/(1 + \rho_2 H_r)r^* \end{aligned} \tag{2.19}$$

$$e = -\{r_0^* l/[(X_q - Z_q) - r_0^* l_0]\} \tag{2.20}$$

$$F = [(1 - C_N)/C_w]r_0^*(l + l_0 e) - (C_r/C_w)r \tag{2.21}$$

Across steady states, the domestic level of interest rate moves only if the risk premium or the level of the foreign interest rate changes. This is given by equation (2.17), and it follows from the interest parity condition and from the postulate that in steady state the level of exchange rate is expected to remain constant.

In turn, the level of foreign-currency-denominated financial assets must be consistent with the relationship determining the components of financial wealth, hence we have equation (2.18).

In addition to these two relationships, we have three further equations for the steady state solution of the model. These follow from considering that (de/dt), (dF/dt) and (dl/dt) are all equal to zero.

For a constant long-run level of the exchange rate – that is, de/dt equals zero – equation (2.14) provides us with the money market equilibrium condition (2.19). In turn, for a constant level of foreign assets and exchange rate, equation (2.12) becomes a relationship that states that the current account must be balanced. From this relationship we deduce equation (2.20).

Finally, one of the characteristics of the steady state is that the net stock of privately held financial assets available in the system must coincide with the long-run desired level. This condition, represented by equation (2.21), is a relationship derived from equation (2.13), when the flow of real savings is equal to zero.

The long-run equilibrium can be analyzed on the basis of a system with five reduced form equations, for a given level of government bonds, b, foreign interest rates, r^*, and initial levels of foreign asset holdings, l_0. These five equations – (2.17), (2.18), (2.20), (2.21) and (2.19) – solve for the equilibrium values of the net stock of privately held financial assets, F, the real exchange rate, e, the level of assets denominated in foreign currency, l, the supply of money, h, and the level of the domestic interest rate, r.

2.2.3 Analysis of the Steady-State Characteristics of the Model

Stock-flow relationships

The steady state of the model has a number of characteristics worth mentioning. One of them is that capital gains and losses are zero and the component C^a – the variations in the autonomous component of private expenditure – is constrained to be zero. Hence, substituting for r in the consumption function (2.4) and using (2.21) to solve for F, we get the following equation determining the variations in the level of consumption across steady states:

$$C = r_0^*(l + l_o e) \tag{2.22}$$

This equation states that the long-run propensity to spend out of disposable income is one. That is, across steady states changes in private expenditure must be equal to the changes in the level of private disposable income. *Ex hypothesis* interest earnings on foreign assets is the only determinant of change in disposable income. GDP is constant throughout the analysis and variations in interest earnings on government bonds are taxed away.

We specified the model in such a way that throughout the analysis, including the steady state, the level of GDP does not differ from its predisturbance level. Hence Y in equation (2.2) equals zero. This result can be considered the counterpart of the policy rule for public expenditure stated by equation (2.6). This policy rule can also be interpreted as stating that the changes in the level of public expenditure across steady states will be zero if the changes in the level of consumption are of the same magnitude, but of opposite sign to the changes in net exports.

Consider now the function representing the long-run desired level of the net stock of privately held financial assets – that is, equation (2.21). The following implications can be deduced from this relationship.

First, due to the 'disposable income effect,' the private sector will demand a higher level of financial wealth in those cases in which interest earnings on the stock of foreign assets increase. Moreover there is a given stock-flow relationship between the net stock of financial assets held by the private sector and its disposable income, for those cases in which the level of the domestic interest rate is not affected. This relationship is:

$$(F/C) = [(1 - C_N)/C_w]$$

Second, a *ceteris paribus* permanent decrease in the real level of interest rate – for example, because of a lower risk-premium – induces a reduction in the long-run desired level of the net stock of privately held financial assets. That is, due to the 'real interest rate effect' exclusively, the desired level of financial wealth will be lower.

An insightful way to analyze which one of these two effects dominates, as well as other characteristics of our model, is to consider the way in which a change in the cumulative sum of fiscal deficits – that is, $(b + h)$ – is related to the risk-premium and to other endogenous variables of the model. This analysis is presented next.

Here, we point out an interesting characteristic of the model: in the general case in which the domestic level of interest rate changes in response to a different risk-premium, a *parameter* determines a stock-flow relationship between the net stock of financial assets held by the private sector and its disposable income. This relationship will be shown to be:

$$F/C = [(1 - C_N)/C_w] + [C_r/(C_w H_r r_o^*)][(\beta H_w - \Omega)/(\beta - 1)]$$

Where the parameters β and Ω will be deduced below.

Effects of domestic public indebtedness on privately held financial assets and on the level of the exchange rate

With a flexible exchange rate regime, and current account deficits financed by the private sector exclusively, the variations in the level of the supply of money and of government bonds occur as a result of unbalanced fiscal budgets. This implies that the *sum* of changes in government bonds and money $(b + h)$, must necessarily correspond to the *cumulative* sum of fiscal deficits along the transition between the predisturbance equilibrium situation and the new long-run equilibrium.[7]

We can restate our equations (2.17), (2.18), (2.19), (2.20) and (2.21) as follows, in order to present our model in terms of effects attributed to the long-run implications of the total sequence of fiscal imbalances:

$$r = [(H_w\beta - \Omega)/H_r](b + h) + r^* \quad \beta \leq \Omega/H_w \qquad (2.17a)$$

$$l = -(1 - \beta)(b + h) - l_0 e \qquad (2.18a)$$

$$h = \Omega(b + h) \qquad (2.19a)$$

$$e = -[r_0^*/(X_q - Z_q)]F + [r_0^*/(X_q - Z_q)](b + h) \qquad (2.20a)$$

$$F = \beta(b + h) \qquad \beta < 1 \qquad (2.21a)$$

Considering the money market equilibrium condition (2.19), using (2.17) we can deduce that this market clears when the variation in the long-run level of the domestic interest rate is given by:

$$r = -(H_w/H_r)F + (1/H_r)h$$

This relationship implies a compatibility requirement: namely that the level of interest rate at which the money market clears must not differ from the level determined by the interest rate parity condition represented by (2.17). This consistency is achieved by means of a restriction in the share of the fiscal deficit that, in the transition to the steady state, is financed by money. That is, it is by means of a constraint on the value of Ω in equation (2.15) that the variable h, which represents the deviations of the supply of money with respect to a predisturbance level, becomes an endogenously determined variable that fulfills the above mentioned compatibility requirement.[8] The constraint on the value of Ω is given by:

$$\Omega = \alpha_1\beta - \alpha_2 \qquad (2.23)$$

where:

$$\alpha_1 = \left[H_w + H_r(\rho_1 + \rho_2)\right]\big/(1 + H_r\rho_2)$$
$$\alpha_2 = (H_r\rho_1)\big/(1 + H_r\rho_2) \qquad (2.24)$$

and:

$$\beta = -\frac{(1 - C_N)r_0^* - C_r\rho_1 + (C_r\rho_2\alpha_2)}{C_w + C_r\rho_2 - C_r\rho_2\alpha_1) - (1 - C_w)r_0^* + C_r\rho_1} \qquad (2.25)$$

We represent the parameters α_1 and α_2 with a positive value. For this to be the case, the following inequality must hold:

$$(1 + H_r\rho_2) > 0$$

This inequality is included because of its implications for the equation determining the expected rate of variation in the level of the exchange rate. It ensures that an initial increase in the supply of money resulting from an open market operation induces an instantaneous decline of the domestic interest rate and an expected appreciation of the exchange rate. That is, from the financing rule of the public sector (2.15) the long-run money supply function can be deduced to be $h = \Omega(b + h)$. In turn, given the demand for money and the money market equilibrium – relationship (2.14) – it is possible to solve for Ω as a function of the parameters of the model.

We concentrate on those cases in which the level of foreign interest rate is constant – that is r^* in (2.17a) is assumed to be zero. Hence, long-run reductions in the level of the domestic interest rate are attributed exclusively to the smaller risk premium implied by a reduction in domestic public indebtedness, viz. reductions in $(b + h)$.

Given the demand for money and the financing rule of the public sector – as represented by (2.15) – we can restate the money market equilibrium (2.19) by (2.19a) provided that Ω is given by the value stated by equation (2.23), a constraint we have imposed on the financing behavior of the public sector.

Equation (2.18) indicates that the long-run level of the net stock of privately-held financial assets must be equal to the sum of its components. Using this equation we can substitute for $(l + l_0 e)$ in

(2.20) in order to restate it by (2.20a).

Equation (2.21a) follows from (2.21) after a number of substitutions, using the value of β, which is defined by (2.25). With (2.21a) we can restate as (2.18a).

When stocks and flows – F and C – move in the same direction, it is inferred that the disposable income effect on the demand for net stock of financial assets is not outweighed by the real interest rate effect. Whether this will be the case depends on the value of β in (2.21a), to be discussed below. (Notice that stock-flow relationship between the net stock of financial assets held by the private sector and its disposable income can be represented by $\beta/r^*(\beta - 1)$.)

The value of β in equation (2.21a) is negative in those cases in which the above-mentioned disposable income effect dominates the interest rate effect on the demand for the net stock of privately held financial assets. This will be the case where domestic and foreign non-monetary assets are close or very close substitutes in private portfolios – a case captured in this model with lower values of ρ in the equation determining risk premium (2.10). On the other hand, in those cases in which a reduction in public indebtedness reduces the domestic interest rate to such an extent as to outweigh disposable income effects, β will be positive.

To deduce the value of β in equation (2.21a), we first use equations (2.17), (2.20) and (2.19) to solve for the levels or disposable income and interest rate in equation (2.21) – which determines the level of the net stock of privately held financial assets. From this substitution we get:

$$F = -\left(\frac{(1 - C_N)r_0^* - C_r\rho_1}{C_w + C_r\rho_2 - C_r\rho_2\alpha_1}\right)\left(\frac{X_q - Z_q}{r_0^*}\right)e$$
$$-\left(\frac{(C_r\rho_2 H_r\rho_1)}{(C_w + C_r\rho_2 - C_r\rho_2\alpha_1)(1 + H_r\rho_2)}\right)(b + h) \quad (2.26)$$

The resulting equation, together with the relationship determining a balanced current account – equation (2.20a) – constitute a semi-reduced form system of two equations determining the equilibrium values of e and F for given values of the cumulative sum of fiscal deficits $(b + h)$. In order to consider how the variables F and $(b + h)$ are related, we use these two equations to get:

$$F = -\left(\frac{(1 - C_N)r_0^* - C_r\rho_1 + (C_r\rho_2\alpha_2)}{(C_w + C_r\rho_2 - C_r\rho_2\alpha_1) - (1 - C_N)r_0^* + C_r\rho_1}\right)(b + h) \quad (2.27)$$

Now consider equation (2.20a). From this equation and (2.21a), it follows that for values of β less than one, the effect of a reduction in long-run domestic public indebtedness is a real exchange rate appreciation (that is, $b + h$ is positively related to e).

In turn, the condition ensuring a value of β less than one is:

$$(1 - C_N)r^* < C_w \quad (2.28)$$

In the final section we identify this condition among the saddle-point requirements of the model. That is, we find this inequality to be among the conditions that determine that the model has only one unstable root, thereby ensuring that, after an initial jump of the exchange rate, the system converges to its steady state.

Notice that when this condition holds, the denominator of β in (2.25) is positive. The sign of the numerator, in turn, is determined by the parameters representing the degree of asset substitutability – that is, the ρ. In other words, the value of β is negative for relatively low values of ρ.

A graphical analysis

From our analysis, it follows that the effect of a reduction in long-run domestic public indebtedness is a real exchange rate appreciation. We now rely on a graphical analysis to consider its effects on the net stock of privately held financial assets.

Equation (2.26) can be considered to be a relationship determining the combination of long-run equilibrium levels of e and F at which the available level of the net stock of privately held financial assets is equal to the long-run desired level by the private sector for given values of $(b + h)$. In turn, through rearranging terms, equation (2.20a) can be represented by:

$$F = -\left[\frac{(X_q - Z_q)}{r_0^*}\right]e + (b + h) \quad (2.29)$$

By means of equation (2.29) we represent in Figure 2.1 the schedule *EE*. This schedule determines the combination of long-run equilibrium values of e and F for which the current account is

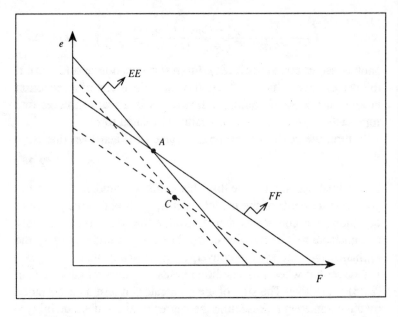

Figure 2.1   Effects of a change in domestic public debt on the real level of
exchange rate and privately held financial assets

balanced for given values of $(b + h)$. The slope of the *EE* schedule
is unambiguously negative.

In Figure 2.1 we also represent, using (2.26), the *FF* schedule as
a negatively sloped relation. We concentrate on the case in which
the slope of the *FF* is negative. We follow this procedure because,
as will be shown in the final section, in this case the sufficient
requirements for the saddle-point stability conditions of the model
are fulfilled. The two conditions determining a negatively signed
slope for the schedule refer to cases in which either non-monetary
assets are perfect substitutes or the degree of imperfect
substitutability is moderate. These conditions are:

$$\rho_2 < -(C_w/C_r) \tag{2.30}$$

$$-\rho_1 < -[(1 - C_N)/C_r] \tag{2.31}$$

These conditions establish a limit for the sensitivity of parameters
that determine how the risk premium on domestic assets changes
when the composition of assets in the portfolio changes.

Based first on (2.30), we define cases with a low degree of

imperfect asset substitutability as those in which the parameter representing the sensitivity of the risk premium to the variations in the level of government bonds in the portfolio, ρ_2, is smaller than another parameter. This latter parameter is given by the inverse of the partial derivative of the long-run desired net stock of privately held financial assets with respect to the real level of the domestic interest rate, which is equal to $-C_w/C_r$.

In turn condition (2.21) enables us to establish an upper limit for the absolute value of the sensitivity of the risk premium to changes in the level of foreign assets, $-\rho_1$. This limit can be specified in terms of partial derivatives of the long-run desired level of the net stock of privately held financial assets and of the foreign level of interest rate.

The absolute value of slope of the *FF* schedule is smaller than corresponding one of the *EE* schedule – as it is represented in Figure 2.1 – when the following inequality holds:

$$\frac{C_w + C_r\rho_2 - C_r\rho_2\alpha_1}{(1 - C_N)r_0^* - C_r\rho_1} > 1 \tag{2.32}$$

When (2.21) holds, the denominator of inequality (2.32) is positive. Hence this latter inequality can be restated as:

$$\left(\frac{C_r}{C_w}\right)(\rho_2 + \rho_1) - \left(\frac{C_r\rho_2\alpha_1}{C_w}\right) > \left[\frac{(1 - C_N)r_0^*}{C_w}\right] - 1$$

The left-hand side of this inequality has a positive value. In turn, the right-hand side has a negative value, since a sufficient condition for this to be the case is (2.28), a stability requirement that we assume to hold. (The parameter determining the sensitivity of the risk premium to variations in the level of foreign assets, ρ_1, is negative and greater in absolute value than ρ_2, the parameter related to variations in the level of government bonds.)

According to equations (2.29) and (2.26), both schedules shift to the left when the cumulative sum of fiscal deficits decreases. Consider an initial point *A* in Figure 2.1. For the size of the shift of the *FF* schedule to be larger in absolute magnitude than the size of the shift of the *EE* schedule, and hence for the new long-run equilibrium to be at point *C* in the figure, the following requirement must be fulfilled:[9]

$$-[(C_r\rho_2\alpha_2)/(C_w + C_r\rho_2 - C_r\rho_2\alpha_1)] < 1 \qquad (2.33)$$

Substituting for α_1 and α_2 as stated in (2.24) and simplifying terms, these requirements can be represented by:

$$\rho_2 < -[(C_w/C_r)][(1 + H_r\rho_2)/(1 - H_w)] \qquad (2.34)$$

By means of (2.30), an upper limit for the sensitivity of risk premium to the changes to domestic-currency-denominated assets was specified. In addition to this condition, (2.34) is satisfied, provided that the following inequality holds as well:

$$-(H_w/H_r) < -(C_w/C_r) \qquad (2.35)$$

This condition, as shown in the the final section, constitutes one of the requirements ensuring that the long-run equilibrium of the model has the required saddle-point characteristics.

In order to consider the sign of β in equation (2.25), we firstly point out that the denominator of this parameter is positive in those cases in which the slope of the FF schedule is smaller in absolute value than the slope of the EE schedule. Hence, after rearranging terms, we deduce that the combination of parameters implying that the variables F and $(b + h)$ are negatively related across steady states is:

$$[(C_r\rho_1)/(1 + H_r\rho_2)] < (1 - C_N)\gamma_0^* \qquad (2.36)$$

This inequality can be re-expressed by:

$$-\rho_1 < -[(1 - C_N)/C_r]r_0^*(1 + H_r\rho_2) \qquad (2.37)$$

Comparing (2.31) with (2.37), we can infer that the latter requires a lower sensitivity of risk-premium than the former since the combination of parameters $H_r\rho_2$ – although less than one in absolute terms – has a negative sign.

We conclude that the value of β in (2.25) is negative when non-monetary assets are not such imperfect substitutes so as to violate conditions (2.37) or (2.30). Under these conditions, the changes in the real level of domestic public indebtedness and the variations in the real level of the net stock of privately held financial assets are negative related across steady states. That is, the 'income effect' on the demand for financial wealth by the private sector dominates the 'interest rate effect'.

2.3 DYNAMIC ANALYSIS RESULTING FROM PRIVATE DISSAVINGS CUM CONTRACTIONARY FISCAL POLICIES

2.3.1 The Mundell–Fleming Results and the Monotonic Convergence Path to the Long-run Equilibrium

With an unaltered level of GDP, a reduction in the level of domestic absorption must be the counterpart of an increase in net exports corresponding to an exchange rate depreciation.

Hence, if on impact a fiscal contraction is not more than compensated by an increase in private expenditure, then a current account surplus via an exchange rate depreciation occurs. This is the standard Mundell–Fleming result.

In turn, as shown in Figure 2.1, the long-run effects of a fiscal contraction that originates a reduction in the level of domestic-currency-denominated assets is an appreciation of the real level of the exchange rate and a lower level of foreign assets.

In Figure 2.2 we represent a monotonic path through which the real exchange rate reaches its long-run equilibrium. The predisturbance equilibrium position is identified to be point *A*.

The shock to the system produces on impact a jump depreciation of the real level of the exchange rate, which displaces the economy to an initial point of the stable manifold, *B*.

Since the model has saddle-point properties, the economy moves along the stable manifold towards point *C*, which corresponds to the new steady state of the system.

Along the transition to a new long-run equilibrium surplus in current account increase the level of foreign assets and fiscal surplus reduce the level of the domestic-currency denominated assets.

As indicated by Figure 2.1, the long-run effect of a fiscal contraction that decreases the level of of domestic debt is a lower level of the net stock of privately-held financial assets. Hence at a new steady state the absolute value of the increase in assets due to the cumulative sum of current account surplus exceeds the value of the reduction in assets due to the cumulative sum of fiscal surplus.

When assets are not perfect substitutes, the risk premium changes across steady states as a result of the variation in the composition of financial assets. Therefore, in the case under

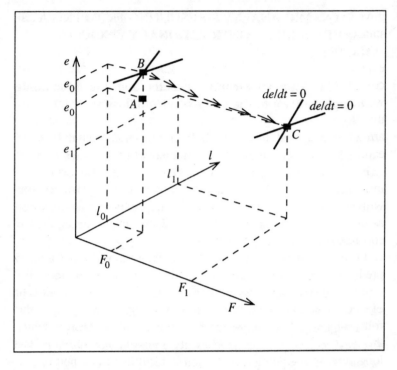

Figure 2.2   Monotonic trajectory of the real exchange rate

consideration the long-run level of the domestic interest rate decreases.

In this analysis the level of GDP does not change. In addition, changes in interest earnings on government bonds are taxed away. This implies that for a zero fiscal surplus in the new steady state the level of public expenditure must return to its predisturbance level. For this to be the case – as represented by equation (2.6) – changes in net exports must be equal in magnitude, but opposite in sign to the changes in private expenditure.

Sachs and Wyplosz (1984) pointed out an interesting implication that follows from the requirement of a long-run balance between the flows of income and expenditure corresponding to the public sector, that is, of a zero fiscal surplus. At a new steady state the level of public expenditure must return to its predisturbance situation, but in addition taxes must be modified in order to compensate for changes in interest payments on government bonds. For this reason, they argued that 'the fiscal stance in the steady state is the *opposite* of the initial move...'[10]

On the other hand, the long-run changes in the level of expenditure and of the disposable income of the private sector must coincide. Otherwise the net stock of privately held financial assets would not be constant. We have incorporated a set of assumptions that imply that the long-run changes in private disposable income are of equal magnitude and sign to the variations in interest earnings on assets denominated in foreign currency.

In turn, the variation in net exports must match the changes in interest earnings on foreign assets. Otherwise the current account will not be balanced. Therefore, with a higher level of foreign assets at a new steady state and hence an increase in the corresponding interest earnings, the level of consumption is higher and that of net exports is lower than the corresponding ones in the predisturbance situation.

It is noteworthy that the inclusion of wealth and portfolio effects of current account deficits induced by fiscal actions implies the following result, for the case analysed in Figure 2.2: it is not only the initial effect on the real exchange rate that is reversed in the long run. The long-run effects on private expenditure and on the real levels of the net stock of privately held financial assets also have an opposite sign to the one they have on impact.

2.3.2 Impact Exchange Rate Adjustment

A current account deficit will be registered even if there is a fiscal surplus, provided that, as a result of the shock to the system, the level of expenditure of the private sector is greater than its disposable income, and that private expansion outweighs public contraction in aggregate demand. That is, provided that private dissaving outweighs public sector saving. (This follows from the goods market equilibrium condition.)

When the exchange rate is flexible, an initial current account deficit must be the counterpart of an impact exchange rate appreciation and of a capital account surplus. In turn, the incipient capital inflows that lead the capital account of the balance of payments into a surplus must correspond to the financing of the private sector dissaving, which does not have the fiscal surplus as a counterpart.

A point to be stressed is that these incipient capital inflows – which are due to the desire by the private sector to change the composition and size of its financial portfolio – are induced by the behavior of forward-looking agents. That is, the resulting movements of the exchange rate are dependent upon what agents foresee as the transitional and long-run effects of the shocks to the economy. Because of the forward-looking nature of this behavior, reflected in the financial markets, the movements in the level of the exchange rate are identified with those of the non-predetermined or 'jumping' variable of the model.

Hence, as is illustrated in Figures 2.3 and 2.4, when an unforeseen shock occurs, the level of exchange rate exhibits an initial discrete jump from *A* to *B*, to a point on the saddle-path trajectory, thereafter moving continuously until the economy reaches its new long-run equilibrium. Moreover, because of the characteristics of the non-predetermined variables, the initial discrete jump of the exchange rate will occur even in those cases in which the shocks have not yet taken place, but in which the 'news' of their future occurrence arrives.

Interest rate adjustments

An exchange rate appreciation can happen together with either an *increase* or a *fall* in the level of domestic interest rate, depending on the *expected* direction of the movement of the exchange rate. This follows from the covered interest rate parity condition, as represented by equation (2.11). However the movements in the domestic level of interest rates must also be consistent with the clearing process in the money market.

Therefore short-term movements in the level of the domestic interest rate, resulting from unexpected shocks, can be determined in this model on the basis of initial adjustments on the money market. In those cases in which, *ex hypothesis*, neither the level of the nominal supply of money nor the level of its deflator are altered by an initial shock, the adjustment in this market must occur through compensating movements of the arguments of the demand for money. These arguments are the levels of the net stock of privately held financial assets and the domestic interest rate.

Initial positive wealth effects in the demand for money,

occurring because of a downward jump in the exchange rate, imply that this latter variable must be expected to move toward its predisturbance level. That is, an expected exchange rate depreciation must be the counterpart of the increase in domestic interest rate which clears the money market.

On the other hand, an initial decline in the level of the domestic interest rates, associated with an *expected* exchange rate *appreciation*, can occur along with an impact exchange appreciation. This can occur when an increase of private expenditure is accompanied by an initial excess supply of money.

In our model, the real level of the net stock of privately held financial assets at an initial point of the traverse to a new long-run equilibrium can differ from its predisturbance level. This is because part of this stock is denominated in foreign currency and the exchange rate exhibits an initial discrete movement.[11] This characteristic enables us to analyze the case in which an excess supply of money is associated with a decline in the real level of the net stock of privately held financial assets, because the private sector is a net debtor in foreign currency. We suggest, however, that the results can be generalized. For example we can relax our assumptions of no capital gains and losses on non-monetary assets due to variations in the domestic level of interest rate, or relax the assumption that the price deflator of the money supply is not affected by exchange rate movements.

Adjustments in the goods market

The effects of initial variations in the real level of financial wealth of private sector must be explicitly considered not only in the money market, but also in the goods market. The effects on the goods market are associated with wealth effects on private expenditure. As represented in equation (2.4), changes in the real level of wealth have two effects on private expenditure, one direct and the other indirect via induced movements in interest rates. In order to establish which of them dominates, we rely on one of the conditions for the long-run equilibrium of the model to have the required saddle-point characteristics. This condition, specified as (2.35) can be expressed as:

$$C_w - C_r(H_w/H_r) > 0 \qquad (2.38)$$

As already discussed, an initial increase in the real level of the net stock of privately held financial assets induces, via adjustments in the money market, an increase in the level of the domestic interest rate. We interpret condition (2.38) as implying that the direct expenditure-inducing wealth effect on private expenditure must not be outweighed by the expenditure-reducing interest rate effect.

An initial exchange rate appreciation can occur in our model, even when the private sector is a net debtor. For this to happen the following situation must occur in the goods market: an autonomously determined increase of private sector expenditure, C^a, must be of an amount that is greater than the sum of the absolute value of two expenditure-reducing effects – so as to have a current account deficit. These effects are a negative net stock effect, which follows because condition (2.38) is postulated to hold, and an initial fiscal contraction effect, which follows from the assumed behavior stated in (2.6). When the private sector is a net creditor in foreign currency, the induced wealth effect will be positive, thereby requiring an autonomously determined private expenditure of a reduced magnitude to lead to this result.

2.3.3 A Non-Monotonic Convergence Path

In the previous section we analyzed the characteristics of the long-run equilibrium of our model. We concluded that the long-run relationship between changes in the level of domestic public indebtedness, $(b + h)$, and in the real levels of exchange rate, e, was negative.

In a model with forward-looking expectations like ours, this has the following implication: when agents foresee that, as a result of the future use of fiscal instruments, a long-run decrease in the level of domestic public indebtedness will occur, they expect that, along with this result, the long-run real exchange rate level will appreciate with respect to its predisturbance level.

When this long-run implication is considered as part of the case in which private sector dissavings more than compensates public sector savings in the short run, the following question arises because of the initial exchange rate appreciation associated with the current account deficit that this short-run scenario implies: how can a short- and long-run real exchange rate appreciation be possible, given the constraint requiring long-run variations in interest earnings on foreign assets – resulting from a different net foreign asset position of the economy – to be matched with net exports at a postdisturbance steady state?

Our model highlights the implications that this question has for the relationship between initial, transitional and steady state variations in the level and composition of the net stock of privately held financial assets, as well as for the trajectory of the exchange rate towards its new steady state.

The answer to this question is that the trajectory of the exchange rate must be such as to enable the effects due to the initial and final sequence of current account deficits to be more than compensated by those of a sequence of current account surpluses.

The dynamic characteristics of this trajectory rules out a monotonic convergence path for the real exchange rate to its new long-run equilibrium. The reason for this cyclical or non-monotonic behavior is as follows.

On the one hand, we know that whenever the real exchange rate is below its predisturbance level (that is, it has appreciated), the current account is in deficit, and consequently a *reduction* in the level of foreign assets held by the private sector takes place. This is illustrated in Figure 2.4. When the exchange rate is below its predisturbance level, e_0, the level of foreign assets decreases from l_0 to l_1.

On the other hand, since a long-run exchange rate appreciation is associated with a net level of foreign assets at a steady state that is higher than its predisturbance level, that is, e_∞, l_∞, there must necessarily be an eventual reversal of the movement in the level of foreign assets during the transition to the long run (point C in Figure 2.4, when the exchange rate is at the same level as point A).

This reversal must also occur in the real level of the net stock of privately held financial assets when assets are close of perfect substitutes – when the value of β in (2.25) is negative.

For these reversals to occur, the convergence path of the real exchange rate must be non-monotonic, thereby enabling changes in the level of foreign assets owing to a sequence of current account surplus to be larger than the absolute value of the change in assets owing to current account deficits. The non-monotonic behavior of the level of foreign assets and of the exchange rate is illustrated in

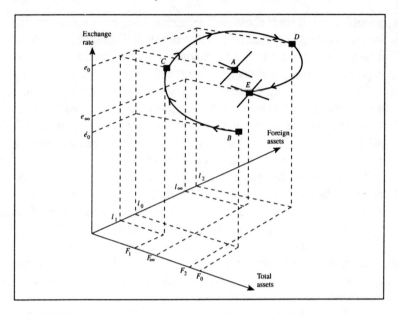

Figure 2.3   Non-monotonic trajectory of the real exchange rate

Figures 2.3 and 2.4.

On impact, due to the forward-looking expectations, the exchange rate exhibits a discrete downward movement from point *A* to point *B* as a result of the shock to the economy.

The domestic level of interest also adjusts so as to clear the money market and enable portfolio adjustments desired by agents who foresee the transitory and long-run effects of the shock. The initial shock to the system can be either an unforeseen event or simply the 'news' of its future occurrence.[12] In both cases the exchange rate exhibits a discrete movement.

With this initial level of (appreciated) exchange rate, there is a current account deficit reflecting short-run private dissavings that more than compensate for public sector savings. Incipient capital inflows finance the dissavings of the private sector, which do not have as a counterpart savings of the public sector. This discrepancy corresponds to the current account deficit and to the initial capital account surplus.

As time elapses and an initial series of current account deficits reduces the net foreign asset position of the private sector from l_0

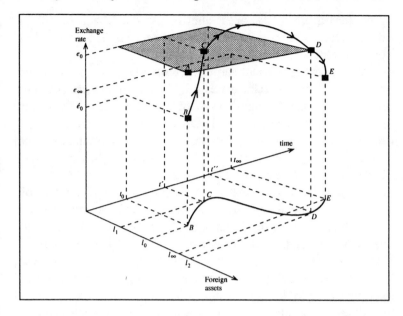

Figure 2.4   Dynamics of exchange rate, foreign assets and private
financial wealth

to l_1 in Figure 2.3, the total level of private sector financial wealth
is diminished from F_0 to F_1. This private decumulation is not only
caused by current account deficits, but also by the fiscal surplus
that occurs simultaneously with the private sector dissaving.

Along with the reduction in the level of the financial wealth of
the private sector, its disposable income diminishes also. At some
point, its expenditure is adjusted downward in line with the lower
levels of disposable income and of financial wealth. This induced
behavior implies that the private sector eventually becomes a net
saver. This behavior can also be seen as the counterpart of a desire
by the private sector to increase the level of its financial wealth in
order to achieve a targeted stock-flow ratio.

For this increase in privately held financial wealth to be possible
– from F_1 to F_2 in Figure 2.3 – the current account deficit must
turn into a surplus.

At some point in the trajectory, the level of foreign assets stops
falling and begins to rise – point C in Figures 2.3 and 2.4. From
this point the exchange rate has not only returned to its

predisturbance level, e_0, but is already above it. This is because a depreciation with respect to the predisturbance level is required in order to induce a current account surplus.

With a current account surplus, the net stock of foreign assets held by the private sector increases. These surpluses are not only required to make the higher levels of wealth by the private sector possible. There is an additional reason: namely to make the long-run exchange rate appreciation possible. This appreciation cannot occur – as stated by equation (2.20) – unless the flow of interest earnings from foreign assets is higher than its predisturbance equilibrium level. Note that this will happen only if the sum of effects of the initial and final sequence of current account deficits of the dynamic trajectory (from point B to C and from D to E in the figures) is more than compensated by those of the sequence of current account surpluses (from point C to D). When this happens, the new steady state level of foreign assets, l_∞ in Figures 2.3 and 2.4, would be to the right of the initial level, l_0.

At the new steady state, point E in the figures, the exchange rate reaches the level, e_∞, which implies an appreciation with respect to its predisturbance level, e_0 – that is, point A is above point E in Figures 2.3 and 2.4 – and, in this case, a depreciation with respect to point B, the initial point of the traverse to a new long-run equilibrium, e_0. That is, there is an initial overshooting of the permanent exchange rate appreciation induced by the short- run private expansion and fiscal actions.

A point we wish to emphasize is that exchange rate models with forward-looking characteristics, such as the one deployed in this chapter, must exhibit saddle-point stability. This implies that one root of the dynamic system must be unstable. The other roots will determine the dynamics of the system when the shocks have occurred. Hence, for a non-monotonic behavior of the exchange rate – such as the one represented in Figure 2.4 – not to be inadvertently excluded from a model, the following is a necessary condition.

The model must have at least three dynamic equations, thereby enabling the capturing of cyclical movements of the exchange rate by means of the two stable roots that determine the dynamic trajectory of the system. The work presented here helps to make progress in this direction, since most analytical models addressing the problem of exchange rate behavior do not fulfill this condition.

2.3.4 Analysis of the Dynamic Characteristics of the System Matrix

The dynamic structure of our model can be represented by:

$$
\begin{bmatrix}
\dfrac{dl}{dt} \\[2mm]
\dfrac{dF}{dt} \\[2mm]
\dfrac{de}{dt}
\end{bmatrix}
= A
\begin{bmatrix}
l_t \\ F_t \\ e_t
\end{bmatrix}
+ B
\begin{bmatrix}
r_t^* \\ C_t^a
\end{bmatrix}
$$

where:

$$
A =
\begin{bmatrix}
r_0^* - l_0(\rho_1 + \delta) & -l_0[\rho_2 + (H_w/H_r) - \delta] & (X_q - Z_q) + l_0[r_0^* - l_0(\rho_1 + \delta)] \\
a_{21} & a_{22} & a_{23} \\
-\rho_1 - \delta & -[\rho_2 + (H_w/H_r)] + \delta & -l_0(\rho_1 + \delta)
\end{bmatrix}
$$

and:

$$
\begin{aligned}
\delta &= [\rho_2 + (1/H_r)]\Omega \\
a_{21} &= (1 - C_N)r_0^* - l_0(1 - C_v)(\rho_1 - \delta) - (C_r\Omega/H_r) \\
a_{22} &= C_r(H_w/H_r) - C_w - l_0(1 - C_v)[\rho_2 + (H_w/H_r) + \delta] + (C_r\Omega/H_r) \\
a_{23} &= l_0[(1 - C_N)r_0^* - l_0(1 - C_v)(\rho_1 + \delta)] - l_0(C_r\Omega/H_r)
\end{aligned}
$$

The first differential equation of the system is given by the balance of payments relationship, that is, equation (2.12). Using (2.14) to substitute for $(de/dt)/e$, we get:

$$
\begin{aligned}
(dl/dt) = {} & (r_0^* - l_0\rho_1)l_t - l_0[\rho_2 + H_w/H_r)]F_t \\
& + [(X_q - Z_q)] + l_0(r_0^* - l_0\rho_1)]e_t + l_0[(1/H_r) + \rho_2]h_t \quad (2.39)
\end{aligned}
$$

A second differential equation is the one determining the variations in the real level of the net stock of privately held financial assets. This is our equation (2.13), which after substituting for $(de/dt)/e$, e^e and ρ by means of (2.14), (2.1) and (2.10) becomes:

$$
\begin{aligned}
(dF/dt) = {} & [(1 - C_N)r_0^* - l_0(1 - C_v)\rho_1]l_t + \{C_r(H_w/H_r) \\
& - C_w - [l_0(1 - C_v)]\,([\rho_2 + (H_w/H_r)])\}F_t \\
& + l_0[(1 - C_N)r_0^* - l_0(1 - C_v)\rho_1]e_t \\
& - \{l_0(1 - C_v)[\rho_2 + (1/H_r)] - (C_r/H_r)\}h_t \quad (2.40)
\end{aligned}
$$

Our third differential equation is given by equation (2.14) in the text, which determines the behavior of the exchange rate on the basis of the clearing of the money market.

We linearise $(de/dt)/e$ by $(de/dt)/e_0$, and for convenience postulate that the predisturbance level of the real exchange rate, e_o, is equal to one. In addition, the following relationship – which holds at any point in time because of the postulated financing behavior of the public sector, as represented by (2.15) – is being used:

$$h_t = \Omega[F_t - (l_t - l_0 e_t)] \tag{2.41}$$

Requirements for the steady state equilibrium to be a saddle-point

Due to rational expectations about the exchange rate movements, the long-run equilibrium of the model must have saddle-point properties to ensure that, after an initial jump, the system will converge to a new long-run equilibrium. Therefore this system of three differential equations requires two stable roots for its long-run equilibrium to have saddle-point properties, that is, it must have only one unstable root.

A positive value for the determinant of matrix A is one of the necessary conditions for the system to have only one unstable root (this statement follows because the product of the roots of the system has the same sign of the determinant of this matrix).

A positive sign for the determinant of A is not sufficient to rule out the case of three unstable (positive) roots. We must therefore consider complementary procedures based on a negative sign of the trace of A and on the sign of the sum of the determinants of its three 2×2 minors.

Conditions under which the steady state equilibrium of the system has saddle-point properties

The following is a sufficient condition to ensure that the determinant of matrix A has a positive sign:

$$(1 - C_N)r_0^* \rho_2 + C_w \rho_1 + (H_w/H_r)[(1 - C_N)r_0^* - C_r \rho_1] < 0 \quad (2.42)$$

By arranging terms, this inequality can be re-expressed by:

$$-(H_w + H_r\rho_2) < \left[\frac{H_r\rho_1}{(1-C_N)r_0^*}\right]\left[C_w - C_r\left(\frac{H_w}{H_r}\right)\right] \quad (2.43)$$

Condition (2.28), presented in section 2.2.3 of the text, ensures that the saddle-point stability condition (2.43) holds, for those cases in which imperfect assets mobility is not strong, as represented by equation (2.31) in that section.

If the sign of the determinant of matrix A is positive, then a sufficient but not necessary condition for one unstable root is its trace having a negative sign. The condition for the trace of A to have a negative sign is given by:

$$r_0^* - 2l_0\rho_1 - l_0(1-C_v)[\rho_2 + (H_w/H_r)] \\ + C_r(H_w/H_r) - C_w < 0 \quad (2.44)$$

This requirement can alternatively be represented by:

$$r_0^* + C_r(H_w/H_r) - C_w < l_0(\rho_1 + \rho_2) \\ + l_0(\rho_1 - C_v\rho_2) + l_0(1-C_v)(H_w/H_r) \quad (2.45)$$

Hence, when the initial value of assets denominated in foreign currency, l_0, is zero, the trace will have a negative sign if the following condition holds:

$$C_w - C_r(H_w/H_r) > r_0^* \quad (2.46)$$

Since the value of $-\rho_1$ has a larger value than ρ_2, we can infer two additional propositions. First, when the initial value of assets denominated in foreign currency has a negative value, (2.46) is a sufficient but not necessary condition for the trace to have a negative sign. Second, with this criterion, the possibility of three unstable roots cannot be rejected in those cases in which the initial level of foreign assets is positive.

Notice that a negative trace is a sufficient but not necessary requirement for only one unstable root. Hence, if it is not fulfilled it does not preclude the use of other complementary conditions. Therefore we can turn to the third criterion mentioned above.

This last criterion, based on the sum of the determinants of the 2×2 principal minors of matrix A, allows us to discard the possibility of three unstable roots in those cases in which the parameter C_w is greater than the product of $C_r(H_w/H_r)$ – that is, in those cases in which wealth effects dominate over interest rate effects in both consumption and demand for money, viz. $C_w/H_w > C_r/H_r$.

A positive value of the determinant of A is a necessary condition for the long run of the model to be a saddle-point. As can be seen from the condition that determines whether this would be the case – (2.43), when a *ceteris paribus* increase in privately held financial assets induces a reduction in the demand for money, that is when $(H_w + H_r\rho_2) < 0$ – the determinant of A will not have the required sign unless the following condition holds:

$$C_w - C_r(H_w/H_r) > 0 \qquad (2.47)$$

The fulfillment of this inequality is also required to guarantee the sufficient condition for only one unstable root when the combination of parameters given by $(H_w + H_r\rho_2)$ is either positive or zero and the initial level of foreign assets is either zero or negative, but small.

Interpretation of the saddle-point stability conditions

A priori restrictions based on theoretically sound arguments can be used to establish that side conditions – such as our inequality (2.47) – must hold.[13] The explicit inclusion of the money market as one of the components of the model, together with its consistent stock-flow equilibrium in the long run, enables us to posit that a parameter C_w smaller than the absolute value of $C_r(H_w/H_r)$ is incompatible with the following requirement:

$$-H_w(C_r/C_w) + H_r < 0 \qquad (2.48)$$

This inequality implies that, if a shock to the *long-run* equilibrium of the system produces a *ceteris paribus* increase in the level of the domestic interest rate, this increase must induce a decline in the demand for money.

In order to interpret the requirement for saddle-point stability represented by (2.47) in terms of its implications for the flow relationships of the model, two issues must be considered.

On the one hand, the explicit inclusion of the money market equilibrium condition in our model implies that the equilibrium changes in the level of the domestic interest rate must be compatible with the clearing process in this market. Hence a *ceteris paribus* change in the level of government bonds, b, induces a variation in the level of the interest rate that is determined by $-(H_w/H_r)b$.

On the other hand, in this model a *ceteris paribus* increase in the level of government bonds increases the net wealth of the private sector. This implies that an increase in the level of government bonds induces a positive response in the level of consumption due to a wealth effect determined by the parameter C_w.

The variation in the level of consumption due to a change in the level of government bonds will be determined by two effects, one due to a change in the level of wealth, the other to a change in the level of the interest rate. Therefore (2.47) can be interpreted as a condition stating that, as the level of government bonds increases, the level of private consumption must increase.

In general the requirement represented by (2.47) can be considered to imply that, if the domestic interest rate increases due to an initial increase in the real level of the net stock of privately held financial assets, the level of private expenditure must increase as well, because the expenditure-inducing wealth effect must not be outweighed by the expenditure-reducing interest rate effect.

When this requirement is not fulfilled, and the combination of parameters given by $(H_w + H_r\rho_2)$ is negative, the model is completely unstable. A shock to the system – or news of its future occurrence – would imply an explosive path for the endogenous variables.

On the other hand (2.47) has the following implication. A fiscal deficit occurring simultaneously with a current account surplus increases the level of the net stock of privately held financial assets. This increase in financial wealth induces a higher level of private expenditure. However, if (2.47) does not hold, a fall in private expenditure could be induced. This fall in private expenditure could lead to a larger fiscal deficit and current account surplus, which would cause an even greater increase in the level of government bonds and of foreign assets. This in turn would induce a further fall in private expenditure and could continue in an unending explosive process.

3 Stock-Flow Adjustment and the Speed of Convergence of the Economy towards its Long-run Equilibrium

3.1 INTRODUCTION AND SUMMARY OF RESULTS

Two components, whose mutual consistency was emphasized by James Tobin (1982) in his Nobel Lecture, are now indisputably embedded in macroeconomic models. First, the specification of the process determining the equilibrium levels of the endogenous variables of the model at a point in time: among these variables is the flow level of GDP, when it is demand-determined. Second, the specification of the dynamic process determining how changes in levels of stocks lead the economy from a predisturbance situation to a new long-run equilibrium.

In this chapter we show how, by exploiting the restrictions that the stock adjustment mechanism places on the lag relations among the flow variables, it is possible to deduce indicators of the speed of adjustment of the system toward a long-run equilibrium.

We also show the way in which the single-period solution of these models, when explicitly associated with the dynamic process, determines not only equilibrium levels of stocks and flows corresponding to that period, but also provides information of additional changes to be registered in succeeding periods. For example we deduce the determinants of the change in the level of GDP between periods one and two as a proportion of the change that has to occur from period one until the steady-state level is achieved.

We demonstrate that this proportion will be larger – and hence the adjustment tend to be faster – the larger the increase in the net stock of privately held financial assets during the second period is, for a given first period increase in the level of this latter variable.

Kenen (1985), in his survey of stock-flow models for open economies, argues that the monetary and portfolio approaches to the study of the macroeconomic theory and policy of an open economy 'may have had one detrimental influence'. After 'paying particular attention to the way in which they have introduced stock-flow relationships into models of the open economy', he concludes as follows:

> [The monetary and portfolio approaches] have drawn our attention in two directions and thus drawn it away from the central issues of economic policy.
>
> Keynesian models with which most economists worked in the 1950's and 1960's were designed to deal with the medium run – with the problems of achieving economic stability over an old-fashioned business cycle. The newer approaches have drawn attention to the very short run – to market processes determining exchange rates from day to day and week to week – and drawn attention to the very long-run – to the never-never land of the stationary state where stocks of money bonds and wealth have adjusted fully. We may have to come back to the medium run of the typical Keynesian model if we are to deal in a useful way with the hardest problems of the world economy. (Kenen, 1985, p. 693)

Our analysis highlights the importance that adjustments in the stock of privately held financial assets have for the determination and speed of medium-run effects of shocks to the economy. It yields a number of insights into the characteristics of the convergence path of a stock-flow model with an endogenous level of GDP.

We present an open economy model, and based on its consistency in the stock and flow relationships, deduce and interpret analytical results about variations in the equilibrium level of GDP and financial assets that are not exclusively related to the short- and long-run effects of a shock to the system.

Our approach enables us to straddle the gap between interpreting short-, medium- and long-run multiplier effects that autonomous changes in aggregate demand have on the level of GDP and on other endogenous variables of the model.

We provide a framework for considering the proposition stating that the mean lag of the long-run response of GDP to a permanent change in the level of either public expenditure or exports is determined by the steady-state ratio of the level of the net stock of privately held financial assets to the level of the autonomous component of aggregate demand.

Unlike the fixed level of GDP models associated with the monetary approach to the balance of payments, the framework presented here stresses the importance of stock adjustment processes in a context in which the levels of assets desired by the private sector depend on a scale variable that changes throughout the transition to a new long-run equilibrium.

In our model the path of convergence of the level of assets towards a long-run equilibrium depends not only upon the propensities that the private sector has to spend out of assets brought from previous periods, but also on the speed at which the level of GDP converges to its long-run equilibrium.

These results are achieved by combining the conventional dynamic analysis of macromodels with a further procedure. This is restating its dynamic structure as a distributed lag model solving for the equilibrium level of the stock of privately held financial assets. We illustrate the utility of this procedure for a better understanding of the determinants of the convergence path of the economy to a new long-run equilibrium.

Since some of the indicators of the speed of adjustment of GDP are only informative when the evolution of the level of privately held financial assets from a predisturbance situation to a new long-run equilibrium follows a monotonic trajectory, we specify and consider the conditions under which these will be the case.

The structure of this chapter is as follows. In Section 3.2 we specify the model and analyze its dynamic properties. In Section 3.3 we relate its dynamic specification to the use of distributed lag models. We then analyze the determinants of the sequential solution of the level of GDP, as well as its speed of convergence, to a new long-run equilibrium. After an analysis of the conditions in which overshooting of the long-run level of GDP can be ruled out, we end this section with the analysis of the stability conditions of the model and with remarks about the way in which the results can be further extended.

3.2   SPECIFICATION OF THE MODEL

3.2.1   Simplifying Assumptions and Policy Rules

Our analysis relies on an heroic degree of simplification. Important dynamic relationships other than those directly relating to the stock-flow adjustment process are assumed away. We explicitly bypass considerations relating to inflation, exchange and interest rate movements, as well as those relating to forward-looking expectations. In addition we assume away effects associated with variations in interest earnings on non-monetary assets held by the private sector.

Assuming price adjustments away from the analysis, rather than merely being old-fashioned Keynesian analysis, serves a purpose. This is to emphasize the interaction between the dynamics associated with asset accumulation and the determinants of the speed of adjustment of flow variables – such as GDP or current account balances – towards their long-run equilibrium variables.

Studies associated with the monetary approach to the balance of payments analyze the factors that determine the path of convergence of stock variables – private wealth, international reserves, money and so on – towards its long-run equilibrium. Their results are deduced from models with constant GDP and flexible prices. Here we turn this set of assumptions on its head: our study considers the case of constant prices and flexible GDP. This procedure enables us to highlight that, in addition to the factors suggested by the monetary approach to the balance of payments, the path of convergence of the level of assets towards a long-run equilibrium also depends on factors determining the speed at which the level of GDP converges to its long-run equilibrium.

The restrictive assumptions of our analysis appear to refer to a closed economy context. We find some advantages in modelling the problem in terms of an open economy framework. Among these advantages are the following. First, the intrinsic dynamics of the model imply that, as time elapses, more assets are introduced into the system. Our analysis explicitly states they are introduced both via fiscal deficits and current account surplus.

Second, by means of *ad hoc* policy rules we exclude the possibility of a so-called 'quasiequilibrium' in which the private sector is in its long-run equilibrium with respect to the level and composition of assets, while assets flowing out of the system via a current account imbalance are introduced by means of a fiscal imbalance of an equal magnitude. With the framework presented here the possibility of this result can be considered.

That is, by relaxing some assumptions the analysis presented here is useful in determining the speed of adjustment in which a reduction in public expenditure leads to a fiscal surplus that is matched by a surplus in the current account of the balance of payments. Although this 'quasiequilibrium' would not be sustainable because of the implied accumulation of international reserves, the deduction of the determinants of the speed of adjustment towards such an unsustainable situation has analytical interest.

Our analysis is concerned with the effects of a permanent change in an autonomous component of aggregate demand. In our open economy scenario, the shock is postulated to be a permanent increase in exports. In order to exclude the possibility of the abovementioned 'quasiequilibrium', it is also postulated that this initial shock is accompanied by a fiscal shock. The purpose of the postulate related to the use of fiscal instruments is to ensure that the long-run equilibrium is characterized by a balanced current account.

The inclusion of our *ad hoc* policy rules and assumptions enable us to work with an analytically tractable dynamic framework. Relaxing these assumptions – for example, including variations in interest revenue on foreign assets as well as flexible exchange rates and forward-looking expectations about exchange rate movements – would increase the size of the system by at least two difference equations.

Policy experiment

The purpose of our analysis is to concentrate on effects attributed to autonomous variations in aggregate demand, when slack

72   *The Role of Private Financial Wealth*

capacity exists in the economy. The domestic level of prices is assumed constant and, to simplify, equal to unity.

We will concentrate on the effects of a permanent increase in exports. When the level of exchange rate is, *ex-hypothesis*, unaltered, and the rate of taxation out of income and the level of public expenditure remain constant throughout the transition to a new long-run equilibrium, this change in exports would lead to a result in which a current account surplus is exactly matched by a fiscal surplus.

In order to rule out a result like this – in which the stocks held by the private sector coincide with their desired level and composition while the stock of international reserves change, (Cf. McKinnon, 1976) – a fiscal policy-induced change geared to ensure a balanced current account must be specified.

This policy experiment is geared towards illustrating a point, originally raised by Cripps (1983), namely,

> how the fiscal system might serve to stabilize the stock system (stabilization of the flow system is a concept which is familiar to Keynesians). The economy is put on an auto pilot – the government can aim the system at whatever [ratio of public expenditure to marginal propensity to tax out of income] level it wishes and the auto pilot will take care of all the monetary adjustments necessary for it to get there. (Cripps, 1983, p. 165)

Fiscal policy

We therefore assume that, together with the initial change in exports, a realignment of public expenditure takes place. For simplicity we postulate that the authorities select the change in public expenditure that, in the long run, would induce – via changes in the level of GDP – a level of imports equal to the level of exports. Due to reasons that will become clear in the section relating to the long-run solution of the model, to ensure that the current account is balanced in the long run, variations in the level of public expenditure must be a share, (T_y/Z_y), of the variation in exports.

Formally, the initial autonomous change in aggregate demand is given by the following two equations:

$$X_t = X_0 + \Delta X + X_e e_t \qquad\qquad X_e > 0 \qquad (3.1)$$
$$G_t = G_0 + (T_y/Z_y)(\Delta X + X_e e_t) \quad T_y, Z_y > 0 \qquad (3.2)$$

Variables with subscript '0' represent predisturbance levels. Variables without this superscript refer to levels and not discrepancies from predisturbance levels. Hence X_t and G_t represent, respectively, the post-disturbance levels of exports and public expenditure. The variable e_t stands for the level of exchange rate.

Since capital gains and losses on assets have been ruled out of the analysis, the level of disposable income of the private sector, YD, equals GDP less total taxation plus interest earnings on domestic and foreign assets, viz:

$$YD_t = Y_t - T_t + rB_{t-1} + r^* l_{t-1} \qquad (3.3)$$

The total level of taxation during the period has two components: a component that depends on the level of GDP, and a lump-sum level of taxes, T_{0t}, which, as will be explained below, will be assumed to be adjusted as a policy rule.

$$T_t = T_y Y_t + T_{0t} \qquad\qquad T_y > 0 \qquad (3.4)$$

In order to remove potential instability problems associated with the payment of interest on government bonds and foreign assets, we rely on two arbitrary but very powerful suppositions.[1]

First, fiscal authorities adjust the level of a lump-sum tax, T_{0t}, during each period, to a level equal to the sum of interest earnings on government bonds and on foreign assets held by the private sector:

$$T_{0t} = rB_{t-1} + r^* l_{t-1} \qquad (3.5)$$

Second, to assume away interest payments on foreign assets from the definition of the current account balance, making that balance equal to the trade balance, we include an additional postulate. Namely that the public sector grant transfers to foreigners that exactly match interest earnings on foreign assets received by the private sector.

Since these assumptions remove interest income from the definition of disposable income we have no need to distinguish between GDP and national income. For practical purposes it can be considered as a closed economy model.

Monetary policy

In terms of monetary policy it is postulated that, by means of open market operations and interventions in the market for foreign currency – to be specified below – the monetary authorities simultaneously maintain constant levels of exchange and domestic interest rates, that is:

$$e_t = \bar{e} \tag{3.6}$$

$$r_t = \bar{r} \tag{3.7}$$

To simplify we set the variable e as equal to one in order to exclude it from our explicit analysis.

In a study of an open economy conducted by Allen and Kenen (1980) a set of assumptions of this kind was used, but unlike us they allowed for endogenous changes in the domestic level of interest rate. The purpose of these authors was to analyze the implications that follow when households attempt to lodge a fraction of their savings in each of the financial assets that constitute its portfolio and the supply of each of these does not increase at the requisite rate.[2]

With this simplifying procedure, Allen and Kenen stressed an interpretation of the way in which the demand for government bonds is reconciled with its corresponding supply. It consists of associating variations in the level of the domestic interest rate with non-zero market excess demand for government bonds.

This interpretation underlines one important property that characterizes the portfolio-balance models. Namely that the equations identified as market excess demand relationships can handle the variations in the level of assets arising from the reshuffling of portfolios, both by private agents on the demand side and by monetary authorities on the supply side. As has been emphasized by Tobin (1982), in a consistently specified stock-flow model this process takes place simultaneously with the handling of the variations in the level of assets arising from savings of the household sector.[3]

The analysis conducted here is geared towards stressing the implications that follow from the handling of the variations in the real level of financial assets resulting exclusively from savings out of endogenous changes in the level of GDP. For this purpose we explicitly play down effects that variations in the level of the domestic interest rate could have in changing the desired composition and size of the private portfolio.

Our analysis will therefore be based on an interpretation different from the one suggested by Allen and Kenen of the way in which the demand for government bonds is reconciled with its corresponding supply. This interpretation must conform with the reasons for a constant level of the domestic interest rate. That is, the level of this variable remains constant because the monetary authorities ensure that a variation in demand for government bonds that does not coincide with the change in government bonds resulting from a fiscal deficit is matched by an open market operation that changes the supply by a magnitude equal to the discrepancy.

This kind of assumption highlights the fact that if, as a result of a shock to the system, the size of the financial portfolio of the private sector increases across steady states – that is, if the cumulative sum of savings is positive – there would be some room for an increase in government bonds originating from fiscal deficits, without this requiring an adjustment in the relative rates of return on the different assets.

3.2.2   Analysis of the Single-Period Structure of the Model

By construction, capital gains and losses on financial assets are assumed away and the rate of return on government bonds and foreign assets is postulated to remain constant throughout the analysis. In addition, interest earnings on bonds and foreign assets correspond with one of the components of taxation. Therefore the disposable income of the private sector, *YD*, can be represented by GDP less the component of taxation that depends on the level of GDP. Using equations (3.4) and (3.5) we get:

$$YD_t = (1 - T_y)Y_t \tag{3.8}$$

Based on the previously described assumptions we can represent the structure of the model by means of the following equations which we divide in four different blocks.

Flow relationships

Private consumption, C, and investment, I, expenditures are specified as being determined exclusively by the levels of GDP net of taxation, of the level of the domestic interest rate, and of assets carried forward from the previous period W_{t-1} and K_{t-1}, which stand, respectively, for stocks of household wealth and the stock of capital:[4]

$$C_t = C_y(1 - T_y)Y_t + C_r r_t + C_w W_{t-1}$$
$$C_y(1 - T_y), C_w > 0; C_r < 0 \qquad (3.9)$$
$$I_t = I_y Y_t + I_r r_t + I_k K_{t-1} \qquad I_y > 0; I_r, I_k < 0 \qquad (3.10)$$

The parameters C_w and I_k which appear in equations (3.9) and (3.10) are interpreted, respectively, as the propensities to consume and to invest out of stocks brought forward from the previous period.

This interpretation is compatible with another one that is based on the relationship between behavioral functions for flow expenditures by the private sector and behavioral functions capturing its desire to achieve a target level of stocks. According to this alternative interpretation, C_w represents the speed of adjustment of wealth to a desired level and I_k the negative of the speed of adjustment of capital to its target level. That is, the consumption function (3.9) is compatible with the following specification for the desired variations in the level of wealth by the household sector during the period:

$$W_t - W_{t-1} = C_w(W_t^* - W_{t-1}) \qquad (3.11)$$

and the investment function (3.10) with the following adjustment process for the stock of capital:

$$K_t - K_{t-1} = -I_k(K_t^* - K_{t-1}) \qquad (3.12)$$

Where W_t^* and K_t^*, using (3.9) and (3.10), are given by:

$$W_t^* = [(1 - C_y)(1 - T_y)/C_w]Y_t - (C_r/C_w)r_t \qquad (3.13)$$
$$K_t^* = -(I_y/I_k)Y_t - (I_r/I_k)r_t \qquad (3.14)$$

The current account of the balance of payments is, under our set of assumptions, the discrepancy between exports, as represented by equation (3.1) and imports of goods, Z. This last variable is assumed to depend on the levels of GDP during the period. Other variables, such as exchange rate, are not explicitly included since we are only concerned with the effects of income-induced variations in the level of GDP:

$$Z_t = Z_y Y_t \quad Z_y > 0 \tag{3.15}$$

Financial relationships

By assumption, the public sector does not borrow in foreign currency and the level of the exchange rate is pegged. In this scenario, a variation in the level of international reserves during the period ΔR_t, is determined by the discrepancy between the current and capital account of the balance of payments. We therefore specify as a variable the end-of-period net level of foreign assets supplied to the private sector, l_t^s. This variable is given by the surplus in the current account of the balance of payments[5] plus the predetermined level of foreign assets less the variations in international reserves during the period.

$$l_t^s \equiv X_t - Z_t + l_{t-1} - \Delta R_t \tag{3.16}$$

Where the predetermined variable representing the net level of foreign assets brought forward from the previous periods by the private sector, l_{t-1}, is defined as the discrepancy between the beginning of period levels of the net stock of privately held financial assets, F_{t-1}, and of the sum of holdings of government bonds, b, and money, h:

$$l_{t-1} \equiv F_{t-1} - (b_{t-1} + h_{t-1}) \tag{3.17}$$

For the current-period solution of the model, the variables represented in (3.17) are classified within the set of predetermined variables and are therefore considered as data.

Due to a number of analytical reasons for specifying the behavior of the company and household sectors in a separate and explicit manner, it is not possible, in general, to represent the demand for the net stock of privately held financial assets as the sum of money, bonds and net foreign assets from two different sectors. We bypass the requirement for an adequate procedure for netting out intersectoral financial transactions between the household and company sector.[6]

This implies considering the private sector as a condensed sector that demands outside financial wealth and the public and foreign sectors as suppliers of it, via fiscal deficits and unbalanced current accounts on the balance of payments.

We therefore assume that there is no market transaction involved in the domestic financing of private investment; households and companies are netted out by a set of *ad hoc* assumptions. These assumptions have been used as a convenient analytical device, but have a number of limitations. Among the type of extensions required to overcome them a number of issues must be explicitly included. Among these are the market for equities, the implications of firms having a long-run desired foreign debt–equity mix and allowing for potential non-permanent changes in aggregate demand arising from the private saving–investment dichotomy.

Based on our assumptions about the netting out of intersectoral financial transactions, we can postulate that because of the stock and flow consistency requirements of the model the following identity holds:

$$h_t^d + b_t^d + l_t^d = YD_t - (C_t + I_t) + F_{t-1} \qquad (3.18)$$

As in the case of private expenditures, we can specify the levels of desired holdings of money, government bonds and foreign assets as being determined by the levels of GDP, of taxation and of assets carried forward from the previous period. In addition we include the level of domestic and foreign interest rates, r_t^*, among the determinants of the demand for assets in order to allow for substitution effects due to relative variations in rates of return. Notice that because of our restrictive assumptions about expectation formations, we do not include expected changes in the level of prices or of exchange rates:

$$h_t^d = h(Y_t, W_{t-1}, r_t, r_t^*) \qquad (3.19)$$

$$b_t^d = b(Y_t, T_t, W_{t-1}, r_t, r_t^*) \qquad (3.20)$$

$$l_t^d = l(Y_t, T_t, W_{t-1}, r_t, r_t^*) \qquad (3.21)$$

In the supply side we define a domestic open market purchase of government bonds as a positive Φ_t^h offset by a negative Φ_t^b of equal size. Along with Tobin (1982), we include an equation relating variables of monetary policy – denoted by Φ_t^h and Φ_t^b – to variations in the level of international reserves:

$$\Phi_t^h \equiv -\Phi_t^b + \Delta R_t \qquad (3.22)$$

Intervention in the foreign exchange market to sell domestic currency for foreign currency assets is a negative Φ_t^h offset by a decline in the level of international reserves by an equal amount. A sterilized acquisition of foreign currency assets is a positive Φ_t^b offset by a positive change in the level of international reserves of equal size.

By assuming that an exogenously given share Ω of the fiscal deficit is financed by printing money, we can represent the supply of money, h_t^s, by:

$$h_t^s \equiv \Omega(G_t - T_t) + h_{t-1} + \Phi_t^h \qquad (3.23)$$

In turn, since the government does not borrow in foreign currency, the supply of government bonds, b_t^s is given by:

$$b_t^s \equiv (1 - \Omega)(G_t - T_t) + b_{t-1} + \Phi_t^b \qquad (3.24)$$

Notice that adding (3.23), (3.24) and using (3.22) we get, after rearranging, an identity representing the budget constraint of the public sector, viz:

$$(b_t^s - b_{t-1}) + \left[(h_t^s - h_{t-1}) - \Delta R_t\right] \equiv (G_t - T_t) \qquad (3.25)$$

This set of financial relationships can be completed with the following two equations, which solve for the equilibrium values of the level of foreign assets and of government bonds:

$$l_t = l_t^s \qquad (3.26)$$
$$b_t = b_t^s \qquad (3.27)$$

Stock relationships

By definition total wealth held by the household sector is equal to the sum of capital stock and net stock of privately held financial assets:

$$W_t \equiv K_t + F_t \tag{3.28}$$

We include in our model a variable representing the supply of the net stock of financial assets available to the private sector, F_t^s, which is identified as the sum of assets supplied by the public and foreign sectors – as represented by (3.16), (3.25) and (3.17). With the assumptions used in this chapter, this variable can be represented by the following equation:

$$F_t^s \equiv (G_t + X_t) - (T_y + Z_y)Y_t + F_{t-1} \tag{3.29}$$

In equilibrium the stock of financial assets supplied to the private sector must not differ from its corresponding equilibrium level. This equation is:

$$F_t = F_t^s \tag{3.30}$$

In turn, a variable representing the demand for net stock of financial assets held by the private sector, F_t^d, can be defined as the sum of the demands for financial assets, viz:

$$F_t^d \equiv h_t^d + b_t^d + l_t^d \tag{3.31}$$

Using identity (3.18) and substituting for YD, C, and I by means of equations (3.8) to (3.10) we can represent (3.31) by:

$$F_t^d = \left[(1 - C_y)(1 - T_y) - I_y \right] Y_t \\ + (1 - C_w)F_{t-1} - (C_w + I_k)K_{t-1} - (C_r + I_r)r_t \tag{3.32}$$

The end-of-period stock of capital, K_t, is equal to the level corresponding to the beginning of period plus investment expenditures undertaken during the period. Therefore, using equation (3.10) we get:

$$K_t = I_y Y_t + I_r r_t + (1 + I_k)K_{t-1} \tag{3.33}$$

Market excess demand equations

The 'flow' relationship representing the equilibrium in the goods market is:

$$Y_t = C_t + I_t + G_t + (X_t - Z_t) \tag{3.34}$$

We have postulated a fixed level of the domestic interest rate. This is achieved by means of open market operations, whose value during the period is determined by the equation representing the market excess demand for government bonds, viz (3.20) equal to (3.24):

$$b_t^d = (1 - \Omega)(G_t - T_t) + \Phi_t^b + b_{t-1} \tag{3.35}$$

Just as the value of the open market operations during the period is solved by the relationship representing the market excess demand for government bonds, the value of the changes in the level of international reserves can be considered to be solved by a relationship representing the market excess demand for assets denominated in foreign currency. This relationship – representing the equality between (3.21) and (3.16) is:

$$l_t^d = X_t - Z_t + l_{t-1} - \Delta R_t \tag{3.36}$$

For given levels of stocks brought forward from previous periods and of exogenous variables, the three excess demand equations (3.34), (3.35) and (3.36) solve for the equilibrium levels of the level of GDP, Y, open market sales of government bonds, Φ_t^b, and variations in international reserves, ΔR_t, (that is, for given initial levels of international reserves, R_{t-1} solves for the end of period level).

Because of our assumptions about monetary policy, these three equations constitute a 'block recursive' system.[7] In this particular case, a complete interdependence of the markets does not exist. Once the level of GDP is solved by one of the equations, the remaining two variables can be solved sequentially by the other two markets.

This particular case enable us to work in the next section within an analytically tractable dynamic framework. The model can also be used to analyze the general case in which monetary policy is different and the non-negligible interactions between the financial and real sectors are part of the analysis. That is, for the general case without interventions in the foreign exchange market or open market operations (for example, Φ_t^b and ΔR_t exogenously equal zero), equations (3.34), (3.35) and (3.36) represent the three markets constituting the reduced form of the system.

In this case the complete interdependence of the three markets would require the simultaneous solution of the three equations and of a dynamic system of at least four difference equations.[8]

Walras' law

By virtue of the consistent specification of the stocks and flows of the model, the following identity holds:

$$(h_t^d - h_t^s) + (b_t^d - b_t^s) + (l_t^d - l_t^s)$$
$$\equiv [Y_t - C_t - I_t - G_t - (X_t - Z_t)] \qquad (3.37)$$

Adding identities (3.18), (3.16) and (3.25) we get (3.37). It implies that, by construction, this model is constituted by four market excess demand relationships. By Walras' law only three of them are independent. The 'redundant' market equilibrium condition is, for the case under consideration, the equilibrium in the money market. It is the equation representing the equality between (3.19) and (3.23), viz:

$$h_t = \Omega(G_t - T_t) + h_{t-1} - \Phi_t^b + \Delta R_t \qquad (3.38)$$

Since this equation is not part of the set of independently determined market relationships, it is not part of the reduced form solution of the model. It solves for the equilibrium level of the stock of money, h_t, given the equilibrium solution for Y, Φ_t^b and ΔR_t.

It can be shown that if equation (3.36) were chosen as the redundant market equilibrium condition and the money market included in the set of independently determined market relationships, this latter market would solve for ΔR_t, and (3.36) would determine the level of one of the financial assets.[9]

For given equilibrium levels of Φ_t^b and ΔR_t, the variable Φ_t^h is solved by equation (3.22) as a non-independent variable of monetary policy. In turn, for given levels of Y, r and e, the set of stock relationships (3.28) to (3.30), (3.32) and (3.33) solves for the levels of W_t, F_t^d, F_t^s, F_t and K_t.

Identity (3.37) is the aggregate market budget constraint of the model. It follows from the budget constraint of the private sector (3.18), of the public sector (3.25) and of the constraint corresponding to the foreign sector, (3.16). Using (3.31), (3.25), (3.29) and (3.17) to condense the financial assets, (3.37) can be restated as follows:

$$F_t^d - F_t^s \equiv Y_t - C_t - I_t - G_t - (X_t - Z_t) \tag{3.39}$$

The relationship of the right-hand side of this identity is the market excess demand for goods. Its left-hand side indicates that the net stock of privately held financial assets equals its equilibrium value when GDP equals aggregate demand, that is, when the right hand-side equals zero.

Alternatively, identity (3.39) can also be interpreted as stating that, given the following relationship:

$$F_t^d = F_t^s \tag{3.40}$$

by implication it follows that the level of GDP is in equilibrium. That is, only one of the two relationships in (3.39) is independent.

Since it is the stock adjustments through time that determines the intrinsic dynamics of the model, concentrating on the implications of (3.40) as an independent relationship is insightful. We will show that, in addition to determining the level of GDP for a given point in time, the equilibrium changes in the level of assets enable us to determine the speed of adjustment of GDP towards its long-run equilibrium level.

In Section 3.3 we will discuss these issues. In the next section we consider the dynamic properties of this model.

3.3.3 Analysis of the Dynamic Structure of the Model

Reduced form of the dynamic specification of the model

The reduced form of our system is constituted by the following three equations:

$$
\begin{aligned}
F_t = {} & \left[\frac{[(1 - C_y)(1 - T_y) - I_y]}{m} \right] (G_t + X_t) \\
& + \left[(1 - C_w) + \frac{[(1 - C_y)(1 - T_y) - I_y]C_w}{m} \right] F_{t-1} \\
& - \left[1 - \frac{[(1 - C_y)(1 - T_y) - I_y]}{m} \right] (C_w + I_k) K_{t-1} \\
& - [(C_r + I_r)/m] r_t
\end{aligned} \tag{3.41}
$$

$$K_t = (I_y/m)(G_t + X_t) + (I_y C_w/m)F_{t-1}$$
$$+ [(I_y/m)(C_w + I_k) + (1 + I_k)]K_{t-1}$$
$$+ \left[\frac{I_y(C_r + I_r)}{m} + I_r\right]r_t \qquad (3.42)$$

$$Y_t = [(F_{t-1} - F_t)/(Z_y + T_y)] + [(G_t + X_t)/(Z_y + T_y)] \qquad (3.43)$$

The variable m represents the inverse of the conventional short-run 'multiplier' of changes in autonomous components of aggregate demand on GDP and is given by:

$$m = (1 - C_y)(1 - T_y) - I_y + Z_y + T_y \qquad (3.44)$$

The assumptions incorporated in our analysis enable us to focus on the characteristics of a system matrix of two difference equations. In particular, they allow us to exclude from the explicit dynamic specification of the model those equations representing the market excess demands for money, bonds and foreign assets.[10] That is, the first two equations of the reduced form model can be represented in matrix notation, viz:

$$\begin{bmatrix} F_t \\ K_t \end{bmatrix} = A \begin{bmatrix} F_{t-1} \\ K_{t-1} \end{bmatrix} + B \begin{bmatrix} G_t \\ r_t \end{bmatrix} \qquad (3.45)$$

where the matrix A and B are defined as follows, after using (3.44) to re-express the parameters of (3.41):

$$A = \begin{bmatrix} \left\{1 - \dfrac{(Z_y + T_y)C_w}{m}\right\} & -\dfrac{(Z_y + T_y)(C_w + I_k)}{m} \\[2ex] \dfrac{I_y C_w}{m} & \left\{1 + I_k + \dfrac{I_y(C_w + I_k)}{m}\right\} \end{bmatrix} \qquad (3.46)$$

$$B = \begin{bmatrix} \left\{\dfrac{(1 - C_y)(1 - T_y) - I_y}{m}\right\} & \dfrac{(Z_y + T_y)(C_r + I_r)}{m} \\[2ex] \dfrac{I_y}{m} & \left\{\dfrac{I_y(C_r + I_r)}{m} + I_r\right\} \end{bmatrix} \qquad (3.47)$$

Long-run solution

The steady-state is characterized by no changes in the level of assets. Hence, when the net stock of privately held financial assets is constant – that is, with $F_t - F_{t-1}$ at zero – we derive from equation (3.43), which determines the level of GDP, that the following relationship holds:[11]

$$\bar{Y} = (G + X)/(Z_y + T_y) \tag{3.48}$$

Given the long-run levels of exports and public expenditure on the one hand and of interest rate on the other, the net stock of privately held financial assets is determined by:

$$\bar{F} = \left[\frac{(1 - C_y)(1 - T_y)}{C_w} + \frac{I_y}{I_k} \right] \frac{(G + X)}{(Z_y + T_y)} - \left[\frac{C_r}{C_w} + \frac{I_r}{I_k} \right] \bar{r} \tag{3.49}$$

In turn, the corresponding equation for the steady-state stock of capital is:

$$\bar{K} = -(I_y/I_k)[(G + X)/(Z_y + T_y)] - (I_r/I_k)\bar{r} \tag{3.50}$$

Equation (3.28) states that the total level of wealth held by the household sector is given by the sum of the net stock of privately held financial assets and the stock of capital. Hence the level of wealth in steady state follows from equations (3.49) and (3.50). Adding these equations and using (3.48) to substitute for Y, we get:

$$\bar{W} = \{[(1 - C_y)(1 - T_y)]/C_w\}\bar{Y} - (C_r/C_w)\bar{r} \tag{3.51}$$

Using (3.51) to substitute for wealth in the equation representing the consumption function – equation (3.9) – and rearranging terms provides the counterpart for a constant level of wealth. Namely, that in steady state the levels of consumption and private disposable income do not differ from each other, that is:

$$\bar{C} = \overline{YD} \tag{3.52}$$

Since equation (3.50) implies a constant level of capital, the steady-state level of investment must be zero.

Long-run determination of the level of GDP

Long-run multipliers were not derived by Keynes. They were derived by extending his analysis to include stock adjustments, stock equilibrium, government and foreign budget constraints and so on. The 'long-run' multiplier of an autonomous change in the level of aggregate demand is determined by means of the relationship representing the sum of the budget constraint of the public and foreign sectors. From our equation (3.48), it follows that the long-run multiplier is $1/(Z_y + T_y)$.

An analysis based on the use of multipliers that are constituted by the sum of the 'propensities to leak out' of the flow of income is related to the Keynesian ideas about the determination of the level of aggregate demand.

Across steady states, as represented by equation (3.52) the consumption of the private sector equals its disposable income, and, as implied by the constant stock of capital, stated by (3.50), the flow of investment is zero. Consequently the private sector has a zero 'propensity to leak out' of the changes in the level of income across steady states. This is one interpretation of the long-run effects of an autonomous change in the level of aggregate demand – that is, changes in the level of income will be equal to the autonomous variations in the components of aggregate demand multiplied by a constant factor $(1/(Z_y + T_y))$. An alternative interpretation is provided below.

Using the investment function (3.10) for the case in which this is zero, together with the consumption function (3.9) when this variable is equal to disposable income, we deduce that the following relationship holds in steady state:

$$[(1 - C_y)(1 - T_y) - I_y]Y = C_w W + I_k K$$

In turn, by means of this last equation and (3.48), after rearranging terms and using (3.28), the long-run level of GDP (3.48) can alternatively be represented by:

$$\overline{Y} = \frac{(G+X)}{m} + \frac{C_w \overline{F}}{m} + \frac{(C_w + I_k)\overline{K}}{m} \qquad (3.53)$$

Where the inverse of the multiplier was specified in (3.44) to be:

$$m = [(1 - C_y)(1 - T_y) - I_y] + (Z_y + T_y) \qquad (3.44)$$

By construction of the analyses, variations in the level of expenditure by the public and foreign sectors occur only during the first period. Thereafter their level remains constant. Hence the total potential effect on GDP of a permanent variation of the level of public expenditure and/or exports can be understood as being determined by two components, as implied by equation (3.53), when expressed in terms of variations across steady states in the level of GDP, viz:

$$(\overline{Y} - Y_0) = \frac{[(G_1 - G_0) + (X_1 - X_0)]}{m}$$
$$+ \frac{1}{m}[C_w(\overline{F} - F_0) + (C_w + I_k)(\overline{K} - K_0)] \quad (3.54)$$

The first one – relating exclusively to the period in which the exogenous shock takes place – multiplies by $(1/m)$ the changes in demand originating from a variation in the demand for goods by the public and foreign sectors.

The second component can be interpreted on the basis of the Keynesian multiplier effects due to 'injections' to and 'leaks' from the flow of income. Accordingly, it is interpreted as if it were the result of an 'autonomous variation' in aggregate demand, equal to the terms in squared brackets, multiplied by a factor, $(1/m)$, the 'Keynesian short-run multiplier'.

Since the second component of equation (3.54) is originated once the levels of G and X remain constant, it is necessarily the result of induced variations in the level of private expenditure. These variations result from attempts by households and firms to achieve a desired long-run stock-flow equilibrium position.

Unlike the first component, which requires only one period to materialize and is attributed to the direct effect of the exogenous shock, the second component refers to the cumulative sum of effects that materialize within a series of periods.

The relationship between 'short-run' changes in the level of GDP and variations in the autonomous component of aggregate demand is given by the short-run multiplier, $(1/m)$. This is identified as one of the results directly deduced from the ideas stated by Keynes (1936) in his *General Theory*. In the analysis presented here, the short-run multiplier refers to the first step of the dynamic sequence, that is, to the *period* in which the shock to the system takes place.

Our approach points to a different reason why Keynes did not extend his analysis to the longer run: that he was concerned with analyzing the effects of autonomous variation in one of the components of aggregate demand on income *only* during the period in which the autonomous change takes place. That is to say, he did not constrain the timespan of his analysis to be 'too short', he simply avoided analyzing what would happen after the period explained by his model.

3.3   DETERMINANTS OF THE SPEED OF ADJUSTMENT OF THE ECONOMY TOWARD ITS LONG-RUN EQUILIBRIUM

The dynamic specification of our model – represented by equations (3.41) to (3.43) – has one peculiarity. This is the way in which the equation solving for the level of GDP is represented.

For a given level of public expenditure and exports, it is the equilibrium level of assets in the system that determines the corresponding level of GDP. That is, we consider equation (3.43), repeated below for convenience, to be a relationship that not only solves for the equilibrium level of GDP in steady state, but also in any period during the transition to a new long-run equilibrium, including, of course, the period in which the shock to the system occurs.

$$Y_t = \frac{F_{t-1} - F_t}{(Z_y + T_y)} + \frac{(G_t + X_t)}{(Z_y + T_y)} \tag{3.43}$$

Along the dynamic trajectory of the system, the stock of privately held assets, F_t, represents an equilibrium variable. This is so because variations in assets supplied – via fiscal deficits and current account surpluses – correspond to changes in the size of the financial portfolio desired by the private sector.

Hence we do not follow the conventional procedure to solve for the equilibrium level of GDP[12] as a variable depending on $(G + X)$, the inherited levels of stocks and the parameters of the model, that is:

$$Y_t = \frac{(G_t + X_t)}{m} + \frac{C_w}{m} W_{t-1} + \frac{I_k}{m} K_{t-1} \tag{3.55}$$

Rather we rely on (3.43) to provide an interpretation of the dynamic equilibrium solution of GDP. This procedure allows us to straddle the gap between interpreting short- and long-run effects of changes in exports and/or public expenditure on changes in the level of GDP.

3.3.1 Medium-Term Determination of the Level of GDP and the Speed of Adjustment of GDP Towards its Long-run Equilibrium

There is an interesting feature of the way equation (3.43) is presented. This is to have information embedded about the medium-term effects that an autonomous change in aggregate demand has on GDP, and about the determinants of the speed of adjustment of this variable towards its long-run equilibrium level.

To consider these issues we represent in Figure 3.1 one possible dynamic trajectory of the level of GDP.

As stated by (3.44), the first period, or short-run, multiplier of $(G + X)$ on GDP, $(1/m)$, is larger the smaller $(Z_y + T_y)$ and $[(1 - C_y)(1 - T_y) - I_y]$ are.

These parameters also contain information relating to the speed of adjustment of the system towards its long-run equilibrium. The following can be pointed out for given values of $(Z_y + T_y)$ – that is, of the inverse of the long-run multiplier: the *lower* the value of the term $[(1 - C_y)(1 - T_y) - I_y]$ is, the *faster* the adjustment of GDP towards its long-run equilibrium would tend to be.

To explain this result, we can reconsider it in light of the sequential determination of the equilibrium level of GDP by asking: what determines the discrepancy between the new long-run equilibrium level of GDP and its level at the end of the first period, Y_1?

The answer is that the total variation in the level of GDP from period two onwards can be deduced by the changes in the equilibrium level of the net stock of privately held financial assets

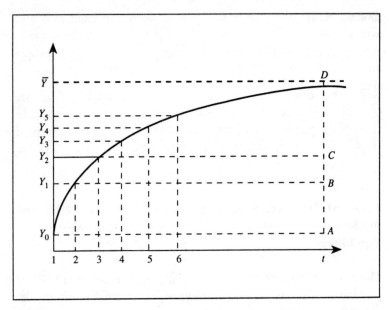

Figure 3.1   Monotonic convergence of GDP towards its long-term level

during the *first* period. That is, the potential variation in the level of GDP that still has to occur from period two onwards is given by:

$$\bar{Y} - Y_1 = (F_1 - F_0)/(Z_y + T_y) \tag{3.56}$$

This result follows, after further rearrangements of terms, when equation (3.48) is used to substitute $(G_1 + X_1)/(Z_y + T_y)$ in (3.43) for the post-disturbance long-run level of GDP.

Hence, dividing the value of the increase in the level of the net stock of privately held financial assets during the period in which the shock to the system occurs by $(Z_y + T_y)$, we know the discrepancy between the new long-run equilibrium level of GDP and its level at the end of the first period.

In turn, using (3.32) and (3.48), the change in GDP that is yet to take place after the first period, relative to the total change in GDP – that is, the ratio BD/AD in Figure 3.1 – is given by:

$$\frac{\bar{Y} - Y_1}{\bar{Y} - Y_0} = \frac{(1 - C_y)(1 - T_y) - I_y}{[(1 - C_y)(1 - T_y) - I_y] + Z_y + T_y} \tag{3.57}$$

Our previous result can now be stated differently, and in a way with direct relation to equation (3.56): given a value of the short-run multiplier, and hence a first period change in GDP resulting from an autonomous change in aggregate demand, we can state that the change in the equilibrium level of the net stock of privately held financial assets during the *first* period will be smaller, the lower the values for the propensity to save out of GDP, net of the propensity to invest out of GDP, are – that is, the lower the propensity to demand financial assets by the private sector as a response of changes in GDP, as represented by the term $[(1 - C_y)(1 - T_y) - I_y]$.

In turn, the smaller the change in the equilibrium level of the net stock of privately held financial assets during the *first* period, the faster the adjustment of GDP to its long-run equilibrium will tend to be. The reason being that the variation in the level of GDP that still has to occur from period two onwards will be smaller.

Moreover, it can be stated that the lower the value of the terms $[(1 - C_y)(1 - T_y) - I_y]$ and the *larger* $(Z_y + T_y)$ are, the faster the adjustment of GDP toward its long-run equilibrium would tend to be.

This is because the change in GDP that is yet to take place after the first period, relative to the first period change in GDP – that is, the ratio BD/AB in Figure 3.1 – is given by:

$$\frac{\overline{Y} - Y_1}{Y_1 - Y_0} = \frac{(1 - C_y)(1 - T_y) - I_y}{(Z_y + T_y)} \tag{3.58}$$

Unlike the changes registered during the first period – and attributed to the direct effect of the exogenous shock – the potential variation in the level of GDP from period two onwards refers to the cumulative sum of effects that materialize within a series of periods.

Given the change in GDP that already has taken place during the first period, by means of equation (3.43) we know the change in the level of GDP that still has to occur in order to be at its long-run equilibrium. With this relationship, and a similar one also based on (3.43), we can ask: which factors determine the percentage of this latter change that takes place during the second period?

The answer can be deduced from the following equation:

$$\frac{Y_2 - Y_1}{\overline{Y} - Y_1} = 1 - \frac{F_2 - F_1}{F_1 - F_0} \qquad (3.59)$$

To deduce this equation, we relied on (3.43) to determine that the potential variation in the level of GDP that still has to occur from period three onwards is given by:

$$\overline{Y} - Y_2 = (F_2 - F_1)/(Z_y + T_y) \qquad (3.60)$$

Combining (3.60) with (3.56) our relationship (3.59) follows.

Hence, based on (3.59), we can answer that, the larger the change in the stock of financial assets held by the private sector during the second period, relative to the corresponding change during the first period, the faster the adjustment of GDP toward its long-run level will tend to be. Hence fewer periods during the sequential dynamic adjustment of the system are required for the GDP to be closer to its long-run equilibrium level.

That is, for a given first period increase in the level of the net stock of privately held financial assets, the change in the level of GDP between periods one and two relative to the change in its level between period one and the new steady-state level (that is, ratio BC/BD in Figure 3.1) is larger, when the increase in the net stock of privately held financial assets during the second period is larger.

Using equation (3.32), which determines the desired changes in the level of financial assets during the period after the shock to the system occurs, the following proposition can be deduced.

Large values of C_w and $-I_k$ in the consumption and investment functions (3.9) and (3.10) will make the coefficient for the ratio represented by the right-hand side of (3.59) larger. Therefore the larger these coefficients are, the faster the adjustment of GDP toward its long-run level will tend to be.

Short-run multipliers

In order to interpret the changes in the level of GDP during the first period, note that, using (3.49) and (3.50) and rearranging terms, the following relationship holds, when the predisturbance equilibrium is a steady state:

$$\frac{F_1 - F_0}{(Z_y + T_y)} = \frac{C_w(\overline{F} - F_0)}{m} + \frac{(C_w + I_k)(\overline{K} - K_0)}{m} \quad (3.61)$$

On the other hand, we have already shown that the left-hand side of equation (3.61) – as stated by (3.56) – is identical to the discrepancy between the variations across steady states in the level of GDP, and the variation in the level of GDP during the first period, $(Y_1 - Y_o)$. (That is, during the period in which the shock to the system occurs.)

Therefore, subtracting (3.61) from (3.54) we can deduce the 'short-run' Keynesian multiplier of variations in the level of public expenditure and exports on variations on the level of GDP, viz:

$$\frac{(Y_1 - Y_0)}{[(G_1 - G_0) + (X_1 - X_0)]} = \frac{1}{m} \quad (3.62)$$

It can finally be mentioned that neither the equilibrium nature of the solution of the model for each transitional step nor its specification of sequential steps as periods of calendar time, are incompatible with Hicks' latest 'reconstruction' of Keynes' theory. Hicks' ideas, however, shed some additional light on the required length of the 'steps' for this conceptual framework to capture the ideas of Keynes.[13]

In a later paper, in which he explains why the 'IS–LM diagram is now much less popular with [him] than [he] thinks it still is with many other people', Hicks (1982, p. 319) argues that Keynes' theory must be considered as an analysis for a single period and, most importantly, that his analysis cannot be reduced to too short a time span. Hicks' points are stated as follows:

> When I did read him [Keynes], I recognized at once that my model and Keynes's had some things in common. Both of us fixed our attention on the behavior of an economy *during a period* – a period that had a past, which nothing that was done during the period could alter, and a future which during the period was unknown.... There were, however, two differences, on which (as we shall see) much depends.
> The more obvious difference was that mine was a flex-price model, a perfect competition model, in which all prices were

flexible, while in Keynes's the level of money wages (at least) was exogenously determined. So Keynes's was a model that was consistent with unemployment, while mine, in his terms was a full employment model.

The other difference is more fundamental; it concerns the length of the *period*. Keynes's (he said) was a 'short period', a term with connotations derived from Marshall; we shall not go far wrong if we think of it as a year. Mine was an 'ultra-short-period'; I called a week. Much more can happen in a year than in a week; Keynes has to allow for quite a lot of things to happen. I wanted to avoid so much happening. (Hicks, 1982, pp. 319–20, emphasis in original)

Some paragraphs later he explains this issue as follows:

If one is to make some sense of the IS–LM model, while paying proper attention to time, one must, I think, insist on two things: (1) that the period in question is a relatively long period, a 'year' rather than a 'week'; and (2) that, because the behaviour of the economy over that 'year' [Hicks' footnote: The *year* must clearly be long enough for the firm to be 'free to revise its decisions as to how much employment to offer' (Keynes, *General Theory*, p. 47, n. 1)] is to be *determined* by propensities, and such like data, it must be assumed to be, in an appropriate sense, *in equilibrium*. This clearly must not imply that it is an all-round flex-price system; the exogenously fixed money wage and the exogenously fixed prices of product must still be retained. But it is not only the market for funds, but also the product market, which must be assumed to be in equilibrium. (Hicks, 1982, p. 326)

3.3.2 Distributed Lag Models and the Dynamic Determination of Privately held Financial Assets

Our dynamic system can be represented in terms of a distributed lag model. For this purpose we firstly rearrange equation (3.41) and represent it as a relationship determining K_{t-1} in terms of $(G + X)$, F_t, and F_{t-1}. By means of the resulting equation we substitute for

K_{t-1} in (3.42) – that is, the equation solving for K_{t-1} and obtain a relationship of the current level of capital in terms of $(G + X)$, F_t and F_{t-1}. Lagging this last equation one period and substituting for K_{t-1} in (3.41) we finally deduce a second order difference equation determining the equilibrium values of the net stock of privately held financial assets, viz:

$$F_t = a_0(G_t + X_t) + a_1 F_{t-1} + a_2 F_{t-2} \qquad (3.63)$$

where a_0 is defined as follows:

$$a_0 = -\frac{I_y(C_w + I_k)}{m} + \frac{[(1 - C_y)(1 - T_y) - I_y]I_k}{m} \qquad (3.64)$$

and the parameters a_2 and a_1, as stated by (3.65) and (3.66), correspond, respectively to the determinant of matrix A – in (3.46) – and to the negative of its trace, viz:

$$a_1 = -2 - I_k + \frac{(Z_y + T_y)C_w}{m} - \frac{I_y(C_w + I_k)}{m} \qquad (3.65)$$

$$a_2 = (1 + I_k) - \frac{(Z_y + T_y)C_w(1 + I_k)}{m} + \frac{I_y(C_w + I_k)}{m} \qquad (3.66)$$

Hence, with this alternative specification, the current level of the net stock of privately held financial assets is determined by its previous two levels and by the level of the autonomous component of aggregate demand – namely the sum of the levels of public expenditure and exports.

By means of equation (3.63), the determination of the equilibrium levels of privately held financial assets can be represented in terms of a distributed lag model. That is, we define L as a lag operator, $LF_t = F_{t-1}$, $L^2F_t = F_{t-2}$, therefore equation (3.63) can be represented by:

$$F = D(L)(G + X) \qquad (3.67)$$

where $D(L)$ is a polynomial in L which can be represented as a rational lag structure. For the case under consideration this structure is defined as follows:

$$D(L) = a_0/(1 - a_1 L + a_2 L^2)$$

This type of model is particularly useful to analyze a process of change taking place over real time. It facilitates the analysis of phenomena in which the effect of a change in one variable over another is posited to be distributed over a number of periods.[15] In addition it reflects a feature emphasized by Tobin, that the model is precise regarding the way to deal with and aggregate time: the short-run equilibrium of the model refers to 'one step of a dynamic sequence, not a repetitive equilibrium into which the economy settles' (Tobin, 1982, p. 172).

From our distributed lag model (3.67) it follows that since *ex-hypothesis* the variable $(G+X)$ remains at a constant level throughout the transition to a new long-run equilibrium, its total potential effect on the determination of the level of the net stock of privately held financial assets is:

$$\overline{F} = D(1)(G+X) \tag{3.68}$$

$D(1)$ indicates the value of the polynomial when L, the lag operator, is replaced by unity. Solving for $D(1)$ – that is:

$$D(1) = a_0/(1 - a_1 + a_2)$$

and using (3.64), (3.65) and (3.66) to substitute for a_0, a_1 and a_2 we get:

$$D(1) = \frac{\left[-\dfrac{I_y(C_w + I_k)}{m} + \dfrac{[(1 - C_y)(1 - T_y) - I_y]I_k}{m} \right]}{\dfrac{(Z_y + T_y)C_w I_k}{m}} \tag{3.69}$$

Further rearrangement of terms in this last equation and the use of (3.44) to substitute for m lead us to the same result as in equation (3.49), viz:

$$D(1) = \frac{\overline{F}}{(G+X)} = \left[\frac{(1 - C_y)(1 - T_y)}{C_w} + \frac{I_y}{I_k} \right] \left[\frac{1}{(Z_y + T_y)} \right] \tag{3.70}$$

Therefore this procedure, based on a distributed lag model to solve for the steady-state relationships, is an alternative to the procedure used in our previous section for deducing the relationship between steady-state changes in the level of F and permanent variations in the level of $(G + X)$. That is, it is an alternative to pre-multiplying the inverse of the matrix $[I - A]$ by matrix B, where I is the identity matrix and A and B are the matrices defined by (3.46) and (3.47).

By re-expressing equation (3.41) as a distributed lag model it is possible to deduce a number of indicators of the speed of convergence of the level of the net stock of privately held financial assets to its long-run equilibrium. Among these indicators is the mean lag of the response of the net stock of privately held financial assets to a variation in the level of one of the autonomous components of aggregate demand. This is given by: mean lag $= [D'(1)]/[D(1)]$ where $D'(1)$ is deduced by differentiating $D(L)$ with respect to L and replacing the value of L by unity.

3.3.3 Determinants of the Speed of Convergence of Privately held Financial Assets to its Long-run Equilibrium Level

As in the case of models associated with the 'monetary approach to the balance of payments', the framework presented here stresses the importance of stock adjustment processes in determining both, the long-run equilibrium of the system and the factors that influence the path of convergence of the system towards its long-run equilibrium. In an analysis of the main features of the monetary approach to the balance of payments, Frenkel and Mussa (1985) have highlighted the importance that a high value for a parameter such as C_w in our consumption function (3.9) (the propensity to spend out of assets brought from the previous period), has in producing a high speed of convergence of the stocks in the system to their long-run equilibrium.[16]

Unlike the model by Frenkel and Mussa, in ours the path of convergence of the level of assets toward a long-run equilibrium depends not only upon the propensities that the private sector has to spend out of assets brought from previous periods. It also depends on the speed at which the level of GDP converges to its long-run equilibrium.

Their analysis – which is based on a fixed-exchange rate model with a constant (full-employment) level of GDP – focuses on the effects that an increase in fiat money by the central bank has on variations in the level of international reserves. Ours focuses on the effects that an increase in an autonomous component of aggregate demand (G and/or X) has on the long-run level of stocks and flows in the system.

As opposed to their study, ours is based on a demand-determined level of GDP. This implies that the levels of assets desired by the private sector depend on a scale variable that changes throughout the transition to a new long-run equilibrium.

To show these results, consider, for example, the particular case in which the parameter corresponding to the adjustment of household's wealth to a desired level, C_w, in equation (3.11) is equal to the parameter representing the adjustment of current to targeted level of capital, $-I_k$, in equation (3.12).[17]

In this case, instead of a second-order difference equation solving for F_t – as in (3.63) – we have a first order difference equation. That is, from (3.41) and (3.44) it follows that for $(C_w + I_k)$ equal to zero, the reduced form of the model is constituted by one difference equation only, namely:

$$F_t = \frac{[(1 - C_y)(1 - T_y) - I_y]}{m}(G + X)$$
$$+ \left[1 - \frac{(Z_y + T_y)C_w}{m}\right]F_{t-1} \qquad (3.71)$$

Using (3.44) to substitute for $[(1 - C_y)(1 - T_y) - I_y]$ it can be represented by means of the following distributed lag model:

$$F_t = D(L)(G + X)$$

where:

$$D(L) = \frac{\dfrac{[(1 - C_y)(1 - T_y) - I_y]}{m}}{1 - \left[1 - \dfrac{(Z_y + T_y)}{m}C_w\right]L} \qquad (3.72)$$

Mean lag of the long-run response of financial assets to changes in the level of public expenditure and exports

Let μ_f represent the mean lag of the total adjustment of the net stock of privately held financial assets to a permanent variation in the level of the autonomous component of aggregate demand, $(G + X)$. For the particular case under consideration the value of

μ_f is given by:

$$\mu_f = \frac{D'(1)}{D(1)} = \left[1 - \frac{(Z_y + T_y)C_w}{m}\right] \Bigg/ \left[\frac{(Z_y + T_y)}{m}C_w\right]$$

Using (3.44) to substitute for m and rearranging terms, this last equation can be represented by:

$$\mu_f = \left[\frac{(1 - C_y)(1 - T_y) - I_y}{(Z_y + T_y)}\right]\left(\frac{1}{C_w}\right) + \frac{(1 - C_w)}{C_w} \qquad (3.73)$$

From this equation it follows that the closer C_w is to unity, the smaller is the mean lag, μ_f, and hence the higher the speed of convergence of the stocks in the system to their long-run equilibrium. This is the result highlighted by models associated with the monetary approach to the balance of payments.

The terms in squared brackets in this equation relate to the speed at which the level of GDP converges to its long-run equilibrium. There are two ways to demonstrate this result. Firstly, by means of (3.58) we can consider what these terms represent. This equation is repeated below for convenience:

$$(\overline{Y} - Y_1)/(Y_1 - Y_0) = [(1 - C_y)(1 - T_y) - I_y]/(Z_y + T_y)$$

As discussed in Section 3.3.1, equation (3.58) represents the change in GDP that is yet to take place after the first period, relative to the first period change in GDP. Therefore the lower the value of the terms $[(1 - C_y)(1 - T_y) - I_y]$ and the *larger* $(Z_y + T_y)$ are, the faster the adjustment of GDP toward its long-run equilibrium would tend to be.

On the other hand, in this particular case the parameter C_w is assumed to equal $-I_k$. Because of this assumption we can re-express the mean lag in (3.73) as:

$$\mu_f = \left[\frac{(1 - C_y)(1 - T_y)}{(Z_y + T_y)C_w} + \frac{I_y}{(Z_y + T_y)I_k}\right] + \frac{(1 - C_w)}{C_w} \qquad (3.74)$$

In turn, by means of equation (3.49), repeated below:

$$\overline{F} = \left[\frac{(1 - C_y)(1 - T_y)}{C_w} + \frac{I_y}{I_k}\right]\left[\frac{(G + X)}{(Z_y + T_y)}\right]$$

we can identify the set of terms in square brackets on the right-hand side of equation (3.74) as the steady-state relationship between variations in the level of $(G + X)$ and the changes in the level of the net stock of privately held financial assets.

This is the second way to show that the terms in square brackets in equation (3.73) and (3.74) are related to the speed at which the level of GDP converges to its long-run equilibrium. As will be demonstrated in the next section, even in the more general case in which the parameter C_w is not equal to $-I_k$, the following proposition holds:

The mean lag of the long-run response of GDP to a permanent change in the level or either public expenditure or exports is determined by the steady-state ratio of changes in the level of the net stock of privately held financial assets to changes in the autonomous component of aggregate demand.

In terms of our notation, if we represent the mean lag of the response of GDP with μ_y, this result is represented by:

$$\mu_y = \frac{(\overline{F} - F_0)}{(\overline{G} - G_0) + (\overline{X} - X_0)}$$
$$= \left[\frac{(1 - C_y)(1 - T_y)}{C_w} + \frac{I_y}{I_k} \right] \left[\frac{1}{(Z_y + T_y)} \right]$$

3.3.4 Determinants of the Speed of Convergence of the Level of GDP to its Long-run Equilibrium

Let (3.75) and (3.76) represent, respectively, the first period and the long-run effects on GDP of an exogenous and permanent increase in the level of the autonomous component of aggregate demand, viz:

$$(Y_1 - Y_0) = [(G_1 - G_0) + (X_1 - X_0)]/m \tag{3.75}$$

$$(Y_1 - Y_0) = [(G_1 - G_0) + (X_1 - X_0)]/(Z_y + T_y) \tag{3.76}$$

The total potential effect that a shock to the system has on the level of GDP – that is, its effect on the steady-state levels of this variable – is given by:

$$\overline{Y} - Y_0 = \sum_{i=1}^{\infty} (Y_i - Y_{i-1})$$

That is, the total potential change in GDP is given by the sum of variations in the level of GDP corresponding to all the periods which the system requires to reach its new long-run equilibrium.

In turn, the mean lag of the total response of GDP to a permanent change in the level of either public expenditure or exports is given, by definition, by the following formula:

$$\mu_y \equiv \frac{[0(Y_1 - Y_0) + \Sigma_{t=1}^{\infty} t(Y_{t+1} - Y_t)]}{(\overline{Y} - Y_0)} \tag{3.77}$$

The mean lag of the long-run response of GDP to a permanent change in the level or either public expenditure or exports highlights the sequential character of the framework. It provides an indicator of the average number of 'steps' for a proportion of the effect predicted by the long-run multipliers to materialize in changes in the equilibrium level of GDP.

It is a result that refers to an horizon of time not related exclusively either to the short- or long-run solution of the model. It was originally advanced by Godley (1983).

We now present a proof of this proposition.

Mean lag of the long-run response of GDP to changes in the level of public expenditure and exports

Let μ_y represent the mean lag of the long-run response of GDP to a permanent change in the level of either public expenditure or exports. In terms of our notation, we present here a proof of the following result:

$$\begin{aligned}
\mu_y &= \frac{\overline{F} - F_0}{(\overline{G} - G_0) + (\overline{X} - X_0)} \\
&= \left[\frac{(1 - C_y)(1 - T_y)}{C_w} + \frac{I_y}{I_k} \right] \left[\frac{1}{(Z_y + T_y)} \right]
\end{aligned} \tag{3.78}$$

In other words, the mean lag of the long-run response of GDP to a permanent change in the level or either public expenditure or exports is determined by the steady-state ratio of changes in the level of the net stock of privately held financial assets to changes in the autonomous component of aggregate demand.

The basis of our proof is equation (3.43). By means of this

equation we can deduce that, from the second period onward, the changes in the equilibrium level of GDP can be represented by:

$$(Y_{t+1} - Y_t) = \frac{[(F_t - F_{t+1}) - (F_{t-1} - F_t)]}{(T_y + Z_y)} \quad t \geq 1 \quad (3.79)$$

Substituting (3.79) in the formula for the mean lag, (3.77), we can represent it by:

$$\mu_y = \frac{0(Y_1 - Y_0)}{(\overline{Y} - Y_0)} + \frac{\Sigma_{t=1}^{\infty} t[(F_t - F_{t+1}) - (F_{t-1} - F_t)]}{(T_y + Z_y) \ (\overline{Y} - Y_0)} \quad (3.80)$$

Expanding the numerator, the formula for the mean lag can be expressed by:

$$\mu_y = \frac{[(F_1 - F_2) - (F_0 - F_1)] + 2[(F_2 - F_3) - (F_1 - F_2)]}{(T_y + Z_y)(\overline{Y} - Y_0)}$$
$$+ \frac{3[(F_3 - F_4) - (F_2 - F_3)] + \ldots\ldots}{(T_y + Z_y)(\overline{Y} - Y_0)} \quad (3.81)$$

This last equation can be represented by:

$$\mu_y = \frac{[(F_1 - F_0) - (F_2 - F_1)] + 2[(F_2 - F_1) - (F_3 - F_2)]}{(T_y + Z_y)(\overline{Y} - Y_0)}$$
$$+ \frac{3[(F_3 - F_2) - (F_4 - F_3)] + 4[(F_4 - F_3) - (F_5 - F_4)] + \ldots\ldots}{(T_y + Z_y)(\overline{Y} - Y_0)}$$
$$(3.82)$$

Further rearranging the terms of the numerator and simplifying, the formula becomes:

$$\mu_y = \{[(F_1 - F_0) + (F_2 - F_1) + (F_3 - F_2) + (F_4 - F_3)$$
$$+ (F_5 - F_4)] + \ldots\}/\{(T_y + Z_y)(\overline{Y} - Y_0)\} \quad (3.83)$$

The denominator of this equation is equal to changes in the autonomous component of aggregate demand, $(G + X)$. This follows from the sum of the budget constraints of the public and foreign sectors, a result also implicit in equation (3.48), which determines the long-run level of GDP:

$$(T_y + Z_y)(\overline{Y} - Y_0) = (\overline{G} - G_0) + (\overline{X} - X_0) \quad (3.84)$$

In turn, the numerator of equation (3.83) represents the cumulative sum of the changes in the net stock of privately held financial assets, from the moment in which the system is disturbed until it reaches its new steady-state situation, viz:

$$\overline{F} - F_0 = (F_1 - F_0) + (F_2 - F_1) + (F_2 - F_1) + (F_3 - F_2)$$
$$+ (F_4 - F_3) + (F_5 - F_4) \tag{3.85}$$

According to equations (3.70) and (3.49), the total potential effect on the level of the net stock of privately held financial assets resulting from a permanent change of the variable $(G + X)$ is given by:

$$(\overline{F} - F_0) = \left[\frac{(1 - C_y)(1 - T_y)}{C_w} + \frac{I_y}{I_k} \right] \left[\frac{(\overline{G} - G_0) + (\overline{X} - X_0)}{(Z_y + T_y)} \right] \tag{3.86}$$

On the one hand, with (3.86) and (3.85) we substitute the terms in the numerator of (3.83). On the other hand, with equation (3.84) we substitute the terms in the denominator. After rearranging terms we get:

$$\mu_y = \frac{(\overline{F} - F_0)}{(\overline{G} - G_0) + (\overline{X} - X_0)}$$
$$= \left[\frac{(1 - C_y)(1 - T_y)}{C_w} + \frac{I_y}{I_k} \right] \left[\frac{1}{(Z_y + T_y)} \right] \tag{3.87}$$

which is the result we set out to prove.

Precursors of stock–flow interactions and mean lag results

In 1935 Michael Kalecki showed how the mean lag of the long-run response of flows to a shock is determined by the stock–flow interactions of the model, thereby becoming a precursor of the Keynesian proposition postulated by Godley (1983).

His analysis presented a mean lag proposition similar to the one analyzed in the previous section, but for a different kind of problem: the relationship between the *stock* of portfolio investment orders and the *flow* of production of investment goods. We consider here his approach and its relationship to our open economy model.

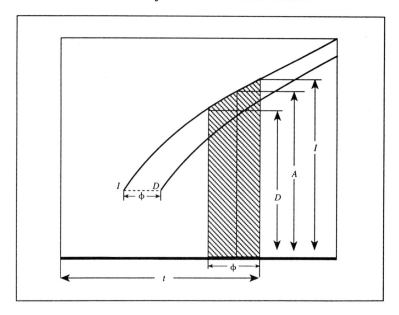

Figure 3.2   Stock–flow interactions and the mean lag

Also based on the relationship between stocks and flows, but
within a constant level of GDP and flexible exchange rate partial-
equilibrium model, Kouri (1983) deduced indicators of the speed
of convergence between the short- and long-run equilibria of the
model. He showed that these indicators depend positively on the
share of the (flow) of imports in relation to the (stock) level of asset
holdings. He deduced two indicators, one is the time it takes to
produce *x* per cent of the cumulative current account surplus
induced by an unexpected shock. The other is the time it takes the
exchange rate to get within *x* per cent of its long-run equilibrium
value.[18]

Kalecki presented his scheme as follows:

We assume that the period of construction Φ is the same for
any investment project. This of course is not in fact the case. Φ
should be considered as the average construction period ...
Three stages should be distinguished in the investment activity:
(1) investment orders, i.e., all types of orders for investment
goods for the sake of reproduction and expansion of the capital

equipment, the volume of which per unit of time will be denoted by I; (2) production of investment goods A which, according to the above, is equal to gross accumulation; (3) deliveries of finished equipment per unit of time D [Kalecki's footnote: A and D differ in that A is the production of investment goods in general, and D is the production of finished investment goods. It follows that the difference $A - D$ is equal to the increment of capital under construction per unit of time.]

The relation between I and D is simple: deliveries D at the time t are equal to the investment orders I placed at the time $t - \Phi$; thus the curve D is the curve I shifted by the time lag Φ (see Figure 3.2).

The relation between the production of investment goods A and investment orders I is somewhat more complicated. The shaded area of the trapezium (Figure 3.2) is equal to the value of orders placed during a period of length Φ ending at time t, and thus equal to the portfolio of orders at time t, which we shall denote by W. Indeed, since the completing of each order takes time Φ, all orders which come within the shaded area have not yet been completed, while all equipment previously ordered has already been installed. Next, production of investment goods is equal to the portfolio of orders W divided by the period of construction:

$$A = W/\Phi$$

Indeed, if each order is to be completed during time Φ then $1/\Phi$ of its volume must be completed per unit of time; thus to the portfolio or orders W, there corresponds the production of investment goods W/Φ.

It follows that A is equal to the shaded area of the trapezium divided by Φ. If the upper side of the trapezium were rectilinear, the production of investment goods A would, at time t, be equal to the median of the trapezium and thus to the investment orders at time $t - (1/2)\Phi$. If the upper side of the trapezium is curvilinear, this will be only approximately true. The production of investment goods at time t is thus approximately equal to the investment orders at time

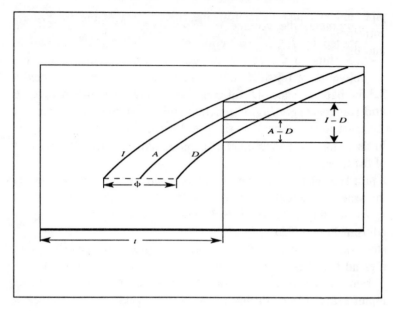

Figure 3.3   Stock–flow interactions and the mean lag calculations

$t - (1/2)\Phi$. Thus the curve A is approximately identical with the curve I shifted by $(1/2)\Phi$ (see Fig. 3.3).

It should be noted that the difference $I - D$ is equal to the increase of the portfolio of orders per unit of time, while the difference $A - D$ is equal to the increase of capital under construction per unit of time. (Kalecki, 1971, p. 3)

Kalecki's diagram is useful for explaining the case of open economy dynamics analyzed in our previous sections.

Instead of investment orders and deliveries, the argument is related to injections and leaks in to and out of the system – variations in the demand for goods by the foreign and public sectors and, respectively, imports and taxation (since these last items depend on GDP).

Instead of a construction period, the parameter Φ represents the mean lag between an injection into the system $G + X$ and its leak out of it via $Z + T$. However these injections and leaks represent variations in the level of financial assets as well, that is, the feed pipe and exit pipe. Therefore the shaded area of the trapezium corresponds to the financial stocks in the system – that is, assets fed into the system that have not yet leaked out.

3.3.5 Medium-term Effects of Stocks on the Level of GDP and the Overshooting of the Long-run Equilibrium

In Section 3.3 we deduced results associated with the determinants of the change in the level of GDP between periods one and two as a proportion of the change that has to occur from period one until the steady-state level is achieved.

We showed that this proportion will be larger – and hence the adjustment will tend to be faster – the larger the increase in the net stock of privately held financial assets during the second period, for a given first period increase in the level of this latter variable.

Here we extend this result. By means of our equation representing the distributed lag model (3.63) and the one determining the level of GDP (3.43), we can establish that, from period three onwards, the discrepancy between the new long-run equilibrium level of GDP and its current level is determined by the changes in the level of the net stock of privately held financial assets during the previous two periods.

To be precise we use equation (3.43), which determines the level of GDP in terms of changes in the level of the stocks of assets held by the private sector. We lag (3.63) and from the resulting relationship subtract (3.63) in order to deduce an equation determining $F_{t-1} - F_t$ in terms of previous changes in this variable only. (By construction of the analysis, permanent variations in the level of expenditure by the public and external sectors, $G + X$, take place only during the first period.) Using the resulting equation together with (3.43) we get:

$$\overline{Y} - Y_t = \frac{[a_1(F_{t-1} - F_{t-2}) + a_2(F_{t-2} - F_{t-3})]}{(Z_y + T_y)} \quad t > 2$$

(3.88)

The left-hand side of this relationship represents the effect of a change in the level of $(G + X)$ on the level of GDP which has not yet materialized at period t.

Using equation (3.56), repeated below for convenience:

$$\overline{Y} - Y_1 = \frac{(F_1 - F_0)}{(Z_y + T_y)}$$

together with (3.88), the following relationship can be deduced:

$$\frac{(Y_t - Y_{t-1})}{(\overline{Y} - Y_1)} =$$

$$- \frac{a_1[(F_{t-1} - F_{t-2}) - (F_{t-2} - F_{t-3})] + a_2[(F_{t-2} - F_{t-3}) - (F_{t-3} - F_{t-4})]\}}{(F_1 - F_0)}$$

$$t > 2 \qquad (3.89)$$

The change in the level of GDP between periods t and $t - 1$ as a proportion of the change that has to occur from period one until the steady-state level is achieved depends, as stated by (3.89), on previous changes in the stock of privately held financial assets.

The interpretation of this result is similar to the case of the second period. The speed of adjustment of GDP toward its long-run level will tend to be faster the larger the variations in the stock of financial assets during previous periods.

We discussed the way in which, by means of the distributed lag representation of our model, it is possible to deduce indicators of the speed of convergence of the level of assets to its long-run equilibrium. Among these indicators we referred to the mean lag of the response to a change in the level of one of the autonomous components of aggregate demand.

As implied by our relationship (3.89), the share that the change of GDP during period t represents in the change that has to occur from period one until the steady-state level is achieved, would be larger during the first periods when the mean lag of the response of the stocks of assets is small. This is because variations in the level of assets tend, in this case, to be more important during the first periods.

For the right-hand side of equation (3.88) to be always positive, and of a smaller value as more periods elapse, a condition must be fulfilled: The level of F must exhibit a non-cyclical traverse process from its predisturbance situation to a new long-run equilibrium.

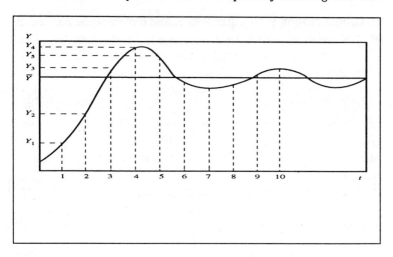

Figure 3.4   Overshooting of the long-term equilibrium of GDP

As relationship (3.88) indicates, the gap between the long-run level of GDP and its current level will diminish as time elapses and more assets are introduced into the system, when the traverse toward the steady state is non-cyclical. This is the case represented in Figure 3.1. In this case the current levels of GDP and of the net stock of privately held financial assets will be unambiguously larger the greater the number of periods elapsed after the shock to the system occurred.

In Figure 3.2 we represent the case in which the level of F_t exhibits a cyclical traverse toward its steady-state value and consequently the level of GDP overshoots its long-run equilibrium.

We deduce below the conditions under which the dynamic structure of the system – as represented by equations (3.41) to (3.42) – exhibits a monotonic, non-cyclical traverse toward its steady-state equilibrium, and hence neither the level of Y_t nor the level of F_t overshoot their long-run equilibrium levels.

Conditions under which an overshooting of the long-run equilibrium of the system can be ruled out

Here we establish the circumstances under which a monotonic traverse of the level of the net stock of privately held financial assets to a new long-run equilibrium can be ensured. Specification of these circumstances is required to assess the analytical relevance of the previously considered propositions about the speed of convergence of GDP towards its long-run equilibrium.

As pointed out by Solow (1983), the mean lag proposition could lose its explanatory power when the system overshoots its long-run equilibrium, since in these cases some of the weights of the distributed lag are negative. As implied by equation (3.88), by ruling out a cyclical behavior of the evolution of the net stock of privately held financial assets we can also ensure that the level of GDP will not overshoot its long-run equilibrium.

In order to address this issue we must consider the characteristic equation corresponding to our dynamic system (3.45), viz:

$$\rho^2 + a_1\rho + a_2 = 0 \tag{3.90}$$

where a_1 and a_2 are defined by (3.65) and (3.66) and correspond, respectively, to the determinant of matrix A in (3.46), and to the negative of its trace.

The case of a cyclical behavior of the evolution of the net stock of privately held financial assets will be ruled out when the roots of the characteristic equation, ρ, are real. In turn, for the roots to be real, the discriminant corresponding to (3.90) must be positive, viz:

$$a_1^2 - 4a_2 \geq 0 \tag{3.91}$$

Using (3.65) and (3.66) to represent this inequality in terms of the parameters of the model, it becomes:

$$\left[\left(\frac{C_w(Z_y + T_y)}{m} - \frac{I_y(C_w + I_k)}{m}\right) - (2 + I_k)\right]^2$$
$$\geq 4\left[(1 + I_k) - \frac{C_w(Z_y + T_y)(1 + I_k)}{m} + \frac{I_y(C_w + I_w)}{m}\right] \tag{3.92}$$

On the basis of the analysis of this inequality, to be presented below, we conclude as follows:

Overshooting is ruled out in those cases in which the adjustment of household wealth, C_w, is slower than the corresponding one for the stock of capital, $-I_k$. That is, when the sum $(C_w + I_k)$ is negative.

In turn, for a given positive value of $(C_w + I_k)$, the occurrence of cycles is less likely the larger the value of $(Z_y + T_y)$ and the lower the value of I_y. Alternatively, we can state that for given values of Z_y, T_y and the steady-state ratio of household's wealth to GDP, $[(1 - C_y)(1 - T_y)]/C_w$, overshooting will be less likely to occur the lower the steady-state ratio of capital stock to GDP, $-(I_y/I_k)$.

Expanding inequality (3.92) we get:

$$(2 + I_k)^2 - (4 + 2I_k) \left[\frac{C_w(Z_y + T_y)}{m} - \frac{I_y(C_w + I_k)}{m} \right]$$

$$+ \left[\frac{I_y(C_w + I_k)}{m} \right]^2 - 2 \left[\frac{I_y C_w(C_w + I_k)(Z_y + T_y)}{m^2} \right]$$

$$+ \left[\frac{(Z_y + T_y)C_w}{m} \right]^2 > (4 + 4I_k)$$

$$- 4 \left[\frac{C_w(Z_y + T_y)}{m} - \frac{I_y(C_w + I_k)}{m} \right]$$

$$- 4I_k \left[\frac{C_w(Z_y + T_y)}{m} \right] \tag{3.93}$$

This inequality becomes, after rearranging and simplifying terms:

$$\frac{2I_y(C_w + I_k)}{m} \left[I_k - \frac{C_w(Z_y + T_y)}{m} \right] + I_k^2 + \left[\frac{I_y(C_w + I_k)}{m} \right]^2$$

$$+ \left[\frac{(Z_y + T_y)C_w}{m} \right]^2 > - \frac{2I_k C_w(Z_y + T_y)}{m} \tag{3.94}$$

Rearranging terms this inequality becomes:

$$(C_w + I_k) < \beta \left[\frac{C_w(Z_y + T_y)}{m} \left(2I_k + \frac{(Z_y + T_y)C_w}{m} \right) + I_k^2 \right]$$

$$+ \beta \left[\frac{I_y(C_w + I_k)}{m} \right]^2 \tag{3.95}$$

$$\beta = - \frac{m^2}{2I_y[I_k m - C_w(Z_y + I_y)]} \tag{3.96}$$

The value of the parameter β in (3.95) is unambiguously positive.

On the other hand, the first set of terms in square brackets in (3.95) is either positive or zero, since it is possible to factorize it and express it as:

$$\left[I_k + \frac{(Z_y + T_y)C_w}{m} \right]^2 > 0 \qquad (3.97)$$

Hence, overshooting will occur only in the following cases:

When, in addition to the sum $(C_w + I_k)$ being a positive value, it is above the upper limit represented by the member of the right-hand side of (3.95).

3.3.6 Stability Conditions

For stability the model has to fulfil the following three conditions:

$$1 + a_1 + a_2 > 0 \qquad (3.98)$$
$$1 - a_1 + a_2 > 0 \qquad (3.99)$$
$$|a_2| < 1 \qquad (3.100)$$

where a_1 and a_2 are defined by (3.65) and (3.66) and correspond, respectively, to the determinant of matrix A in (3.46), and to the negative of its trace.

The first of these requirements can be reduced to the following inequality, after using (3.65) to (3.66) to substitute for a_1 and a_2 in (3.98):

$$-\{[C_w I_k (Z_y + T_y)/m\} > 0.$$

which holds provided that the multiplier $(1/m)$ of changes in autonomous components of aggregate demand on GDP – where m is defined by (3.44) – is positive.

Using (3.65) and (3.66) we deduce that condition (3.99) holds if the following requirement is fulfilled:

$$(1 + I_k)\left[2 - \frac{(Z_y + T_y)C_w}{m} \right] + \left[1 - \frac{(Z_y + T_y)C_w}{m} \right]$$
$$+ 1 + \frac{2I_y(C_w + I_k)}{m} > 0 \qquad (3.101)$$

The sets of terms in square brackets are positive and so is $(1 + I_k)$ since, as equation (3.12) indicates, $-I_k$ is a speed of adjustment whose value is less than unity. Therefore this condition will always be fulfilled in those cases in which the speed of adjustment of household wealth to a desired level, C_w, is faster than the company sector's speed of adjustment of the stock of capital to a target level, $-I_k$, that is, when $(C_w + I_k) > 0$.

In order to consider the conditions in which (3.99) holds when the parameter C_w is smaller than the absolute value of $-I_k$, we arrange the terms of (3.101) in order to represent it by:

$$4 - \frac{2(Z_y + T_y)C_w}{m} + \frac{2I_yC_w}{m} + 2I_k\left[\frac{I_y}{m} + 1\right]$$
$$> \frac{(Z_y + T_y)C_wI_k}{m} \tag{3.102}$$

Dividing both sides of this inequality by 2, using (3.44) to substitute for m, and rearranging terms we get:

$$-I_k < \frac{m + (1 - C_y)(1 - T_y) + [(Z_y + T_y) - I_y](1 - C_w)}{2(1 - C_y)(1 - T_y) + (Z_y + T_y)(2 - C_w)} \tag{3.103}$$

By means of (3.103) and (3.101) we deduce that, in those cases where the parameter $-I_k$ is larger than C_w, the requirement for the stability condition (3.99) to be fulfilled is an upper-bound for the parameter representing the speed of adjustment of capital to its target level.

In turn, condition (3.100) holds if the following requirement is fulfilled:

$$(1 + I_k) - \frac{(Z_y + T_y)C_w(1 + I_k)}{m} + \frac{I_y(C_w + I_k)}{m} < 1$$

Substituting for m using (3.44) and rearranging terms we obtain:

$$\frac{I_kC_w}{m} + I_k\left[\frac{I_y}{m} + \frac{(1 - C_y)(1 - T_y) - I_y + Z_y + T_y}{m}\right]$$
$$- \frac{(Z_y + T_y)I_kC_w}{m} - \frac{(Z_y + T_y)C_w}{m} < 0$$

After further manipulation it becomes:

$$\frac{I_k(1 - C_w)(Z_y + T_y)}{m} - \frac{(Z_y + T_y)C_w}{m}$$

$$< -\frac{I_k(1 - C_y)(1 - T_y)}{m} - \frac{I_y C_w}{m} \qquad (3.104)$$

Finally, this inequality can be re-expressed by:

$$\left[\frac{1}{I_k} - \frac{(1 - C_w)}{C_w}\right](Z_y + T_y) < \frac{(1 - C_y)(1 - T_y)}{C_w} + \frac{I_y}{I_k}$$

The parameter C_w is less than one and positive because it represents the speed of adjustment of current to desired levels of wealth. In turn I_k has a negative value. Hence the left-hand-side of this inequality is negative.

By means of equations (3.49) and (3.48), we deduce that the right-hand side of this last inequality has a positive value if the relationship across steady states between the level of the net stock of privately held financial assets and the level of GDP is positive. That is, the following constitutes a sufficient, but not necessary requirement for condition (3.100) to hold.

$$\frac{\overline{F}}{\overline{Y}} = \frac{\overline{W}}{\overline{Y}} - \frac{\overline{K}}{\overline{Y}} = \frac{(1 - C_y)(1 - T_y)}{C_w} + \frac{I_y}{I_k} > 0$$

In a closed economy, this condition will be expected to hold. As highlighted by Tobin and Buiter (1976) in their criticism of the work by Blinder and Solow (1973), the specification of the model must ensure that the portfolio of the household sector has room for liabilities issued by the public sector. One way to interpret this requirement in an open economy model would be as a limiting value for the level of foreign indebtedness of the private sector, that is, the absolute value of its variation must not be larger than the variation in the value of the sum of domestic-currency-denominated financial assets, when the level of GDP changes.

An alternative interpretation for this last inequality is in terms of the mean lag result presented in the previous section, where it was proved that the mean lag of the long-run response of GDP to a permanent change in the level of either public expenditure or exports is equal to the steady-state ratio of changes in the level of the net stock of privately held financial assets to changes in the autonomous component of aggregate demand.

Hence, a sufficient condition for inequality (3.100) to hold is that this mean lag has a positive value.

3.4 CONCLUDING COMMENTS

Simplifying the dynamic structure of the model presented here enabled us to highlight one result: by exploiting the restrictions that the stock adjustment mechanism places on the lag relations among the flow variables of these models, it is possible to gain insight about the determinants of the speed of adjustment of the system towards a long-run equilibrium.

This approach provided a background for considering the proposition stating that the steady-state ratio of the level of the net stock of privately held financial assets to the level of the autonomous component of aggregate demand constitutes one of these indicators, namely the mean lag of the response of GDP to a permanent change in the level of either public expenditure or exports.

It also enabled us to deduce and interpret analytical results about variations in the equilibrium level of GDP that are not exclusively related to the short- and long-run effects of a shock to the system.

Within a context of a partial-equilibrium model for real exchange rate determination, Kouri (1983) addressed a number of questions that can be considered within the approach and general framework presented in this chapter. Looking for indicators of the speed of convergence between the short- and long-run equilibria of the model when the exchange rate is flexible he deduced two.

One of these indicators refers to the time it takes to produce a given percentage of the cumulative current account surplus induced by an unexpected shock. The other refers to the time it takes the exchange rate to get within a given percentage of its long-run equilibrium value. He showed that these two indicators depend positively on the share (flow) of imports in relation to the (stock) level of asset holdings.

The dynamic analysis of our model can be extended to consider these kinds of result within a context of an open economy model with one market for goods and three markets for financial assets, when it is postulated to have forward-looking agents in a flexible exchange rate regime.

Just as our dynamic system was restated as a distributed lag model solving for the equilibrium level of the stock of privately held financial assets, it would then be restated as a distributed lag model solving for the equilibrium level of the real exchange rate. Since this procedure would lend itself to deduce indicators of the speed of adjustment, such as the corresponding mean lag of the response of the exchange rate, we could determine if this indicator is also given once the long-run stock–flow relations of the model are specified.

Notes and References

1 Long-Term Effects of Fiscal Policy and Domestic Debt on the Real Levels of Exchange Rate and GDP

1. Cf. Branson and Buiter (1983), and Frenkel and Razin (1987).
2. For a rule of this kind in a dynamic model see Sachs and Wyplosz (1984).
3. Sachs (1980), p. 736.
4. Other criticisms are that they ignore the accumulation of physical capital and the issues raised by consideration of the Ricardian equivalence proposition.
5. Cf. C. Kennedy and A. P. Thirwall (1979).
6. If the level of inflation were not exogenously determined, it would constitute another variable that could become endogenously determined. In this case, inflation tax has two roles. On the one hand it finances fiscal deficits and on the other it induces capital losses in private sector financial wealth in order to reduce private consumption.

2 The Dynamics of Real Exchange Rate and Financial Assets of Contractionary Fiscal Policies cum Private Dissavings

1. Other models, for example the work by Kouri (1979, 1982), Dornbuch (1988) and Serven (1990), do not include the issues raised in this chapter, but address part of the second answer by modelling the relationship between investment and movements in the real level of the exchange rate.
2. See Buiter, 1984.
3. There is an additional problem that is not explicitly addressed in this chapter. A non-monotonic movement in the exchange rate that, *ex hypothesi*, is foreseen by the private sector could alter the country-risk, since an exchange rate depreciation following an appreciation is foreseen.
4. Sachs and Wyplosz (1984) and Giavazzi *et al.* (1988), for example, assume that the government closes an exogenously given fiscal deficit at a given rate, bringing its debt to a previously determined target level. Their rule is specified, in our notation, as $db/dt = m(b^* - b)$, where b^*, the target level, and m are exogenously determined parameters.
5. Notice that it is explicitly assumed that the demand for money is not a function of the flow of interest revenue on non-monetary financial assets. Some authors – for example Frenkel and Razin (1987) – have included this variable as one of the arguments of the demand for money, thereby adding a further mechanism through which a fiscal expansion affects the market excess demand for money.
6. We follow this procedure in order to avoid an issue highlighted by Branson and Buiter (1983). Namely, that when the nominal level of the money supply is assumed constant, the long-run level of the domestic price level must change as a result of a policy action that induces a variation in one of the arguments of the money demand function.
7. By construction, changes in the real value of financial assets by means of inflation are eliminated.
8. Notice that the long-run solution allows us to have h determined by b in a direct form. With this relationship we can identify the share of money in the cumulative sum of fiscal deficit – that is $h/(h + b)$ – as a coefficient given by the parameters of the model.

117

9. When non-monetary assets are perfect substitutes, it is only the *FF* schedule that shifts.
10. Sachs and Wyplosz, 1984, p. 9. Their emphasis.
11. The revaluation of the private debt commitments as a channel through which the exchange rate influences the initial level of GDP has been investigated by Frenkel and Razin (1987).
12. In the case of 'news' that shocks will occur in the future, the initial jump of the exchange rate would not be to the saddle-path trajectory. It would be in path when the shock actually takes place. See Wilson, 1979.
13. Note that (2.44) indicates that the trace can have a negative sign even if $C_w - C_r(H_w/H_r)$ has a negative value, provided that the predisturbance level of foreign assets is large and negative. In turn, as stated by (2.43), when the combination of parameters given by the sum of H_w and $H_r \rho_2$ is positive, the determinant of A could still have a positive sign, even if (2.47) does not hold.

3   Stock-Flow Adjustment and the Speed Convergence of the Economy towards its Long-Run Equilibrium

1. The conditions under which these potential instability problems can be ruled out have been analyzed by Turnovsky (1976) for an open economy with fixed exchanged rates and by Christodoulakis *et al.* (1987) for a flexible exchange rate.
2. Similar assumptions to exclude interest earnings on non-monetary assets have been included in analyses such as the one presented by Branson and Henderson (1985).
3. As indicated by Foley (1975) this is a property that follows from the 'end-of-period' specification of the market equilibrium conditions. It is not an implication of being a discrete time model. It is possible to demonstrate that the results deduced with a discrete time model can also be deduced with a continuous time model. Cf. Aoki, 1981, Buiter and Eaton, 1979.
4. Our analysis will focus on the fixed exchange rate case. Therefore, in order to simplify the exposition, we left out the level of exchange rate as one of the determinants of private expenditure and of the demand for assets. This variable would have to be included if we were concerned with the effects of variations in the level of exchange rate on the level of wealth, and hence their effects on private behavior.
5. That is, given that interest earnings on foreign assets are assumed away by means of an equivalent amount of foreign transfers, as represented by (3.5).
6. See, for example, Meade (1979) for a discussion of the kinds of problem created by an *ad hoc* consolidation of intersectoral financial transactions between households and firms.
7. See Sargent, 1979, p. 21
8. Simulation models, such as those of Whittaker *et al.* (1986), consider a flexible exchange rate regime within models in which the long-run level of GDP is demand determined. Our purpose is to have analytically tractable solutions that enable us to gain insight into the dynamic properties of our model. In order to consider the case of a flexible exchange rate regime with forward-looking expectations we need to complement the results of this chapter with those presented in Chapter 2.
9. For a clarification of these issues see Buiter and Eaton, 1979.
10. Notice that a flexible exchange rate regime – whether expectations are assumed to be forward looking or not – would require the inclusion of one 'non-redundant' market excess demand relationship more in the state-space representation of the system.
11. Given our assumptions about variations in public expenditure, as represented in equation (3.2), this equation becomes $Y = (1/Z_y)X$.
12. See for example Turnovsky, 1977, and Murata, 1977.
13. Hicks, 1974.
14. Notice that, to simplify, we ignored changes in the level of interest rate. Their inclusion will not affect our results.
15. See Dhrymes, 1971.

16. Frenkel and Mussa (1985), pp. 692–3.
17. This particular case was also used implicitly by Frenkel and Mussa. It is therefore useful for comparison. Its main advantage is that the mean lag can be more easily deduced.
18. See Gandolfo (1981, p. 4) for the correspondence between a given percentage of the total adjustment in continuous time models and the mean lag of such an adjustment.

Bibliography

ALLEN, P. and KENEN, P. (1980) *Asset Markets, Exchange Rates, and Economic Integration: A Synthesis*, Cambridge University Press, Cambridge.

AOKI, M. (1981) *Dynamic Analysis of Open Economies*, Academic Press, New York.

BLINDER, A. S. and SOLOW, R. M. (1973) 'Does Fiscal Policy Matter?', *Journal of Public Economics*, vol. 2.

BRANSON, W. and BUITER, W. (1983) 'Monetary and Fiscal Policy with Flexible Exchange Rate', in J. S. Bhandari and B. H. Putnam (eds), *Economic Interdependence and Flexible Exchange Rates* MIT Press, Cambridge, MA.

BRANSON, W. and HENDERSON, D. W. (1985) 'The Specification and Influence of Asset Markets', in R. Jones and P. Kenen (eds), *Handbook of International Economics* vol. 2, North Holland, Amsterdam.

BRANSON, W. and ROTEMBERG, J. (1980) 'International Adjustment with Wage Rigidity', *European Economic Review*, vol. 13. pp. 309–32.

BUITER, W. (1984) 'Saddlepoint Problems in Continuous-Time Rational Expectations Models: A General Method and Some Macroeconomic Examples', *Econometrica*, vol. 62 (May).

BUITER, W. and EATON, J. (1979) 'On the Almost Total Adequacy of Keynesian Balance-of-Payments Theory,' *American Economic Review*, vol. 71 (September).

CALDERÓN, A. (1994) 'Fiscal Policy, Private Savings and Current Account Deficits in Mexico', working paper, Colegio de Mexico, Mexico.

CHRISTODOULAKIS, N., MEADE, J. and WEALE, M. (1987) 'Exchange Rate Regimes and Stock Instability', DAE working paper, Cambridge University, September.

CRIPPS, F. (1983) 'Comment on Godley's *Keynes and the Management of Real National Income and Expenditure*', in D. Worswick and J. Trevithick *Keynes and the Modern World*, Cambridge University Press, Cambridge.

DEVEROUX, M. and PURVIS, D. (1990) 'Fiscal Policy and the Real Exchange Rate', *European Economic Review*, vol. 34, pp. 1201–11.

DHRYMES, P. (1971) *Distributed Lags. Problems of Estimation and Formulation*, Holden-Day, Inc., Oakland, CA.

DORNBUSCH, R. (1976) 'Exchange Rate Expectations and Monetary Policy', *Journal of Political Economy*, vol. 84, pp. 1161–76.

DORNBUSCH, R. (1988) 'Real Exchange Rates and Macroeconomics: A Selective Survey', NBER Working Paper No. 2775.

DORNBUSCH, R. and FISCHER, R. (1980) 'Exchange Rates and the Current Account', *American Economic Review*, vol. 70 (December), pp. 960–71.

DREZE, J. and MODIGLIANI, F. (1981) 'The Trade-off between real wages and Employment in an Open Economy (Belgium)', *European Economic Review*, vol. 15 pp. 1–39.

FOLEY D. K. (1975) 'On the Specifications of Asset Equilibrium in Macroeconomic Models', *Journal of Political Economy*, vol. 83, no. 4 (April).

FRENKEL, J. A. and MUSSA, M. J. (1985) 'Asset Markets, Exchange Rates and the Balance of Payments', in R. W. Jones and P. B. Kenen (eds), *Handbook of International Economics*, vol. 2, North Holland, Amsterdam.

122   *Bibliography*

FRENKEL, J. and RAZIN, A. (1987) *The Mundell–Fleming Model: A Quarter Century Later*, IMF Staff Papers, Washington, DC.

GANDOLFO, G. (1981) *Qualitative Analysis and Econometric Estimation of Continuous Time Dynamic Models*, North-Holland, Oxford.

GIAVAZZI, F. and PAGANO, M. (1990) 'Can Severe Fiscal Contractions be Expansionary? Tales of Two Small European Countries', *National Bureau of Economic Macroeconomics Annual*, NBER, Cambridge, MA.

GIAVAZZI, F., SHEEN, J. R. and WYPLOSZ, C. (1983) 'Fiscal Policy and the Real Exchange Rate', Discussion Paper Series no. 224, Department of Economics, University of Essex, October.

GIAVAZZI, F., SHEEN, J. R. and WYPLOSZ, C. (1988) 'The Real Exchange Rate and the Fiscal Aspects of a Natural Resource Discovery', *Oxford Economic Papers*, vol. 40, pp. 427–50.

GODLEY, W. (1983) 'Keynes and the Management of Real National Income and Expenditure', in D. Worswick and J. Trevithick (eds), *Keynes and the Modern World*, Cambridge University Press.

HELLWIG, M., and NEUMANN, M. J. M. (1987) 'Economic Policy in Germany: Was there a runaround?' *Economic Policy*, vol. 5 (October).

HICKS, J. (1974) *The Crisis in Keynesian Economics*, Blackwell, Oxford.

HICKS, J. (1982) 'IS–LM – an Explanation', in J. Hicks, *Money, Interest and Wages, Collected Essays on Economic Theory*, vol. II, Blackwell, Oxford.

KALECKI, M. (1971) *Selected Essays on the Dynamics of the Capitalist Economy*, Cambridge University Press.

KENEN, P. (1985) 'Macroeconomics Analysis and Policy in the Insular Economy', in R. Jones and P. Kenen (eds), *Handbook of International Economics*, vol. 2, North-Holland, Amsterdam.

KENNEDY, C. and THIRWALL, A. P. (1979) 'Import Penetration, Export Performance and Harrod's Trade Multiplier', *Oxford Economic Papers* (July).

KEYNES, J. M. (1936) *The General Theory of Employment, Interest and Money*, Macmillan, London.

KOURI, P. (1979) 'Profitability and Growth in a Small Open Economy' in A. Lindbeck (ed.), *Inflation and Employment in Open Economies*, North Holland, Amsterdam.

KOURI, P. (1982) 'Profitability and Growth' *Scandinavian Journal of Economics*, vol. 2.

KOURI, P. J. K. (1983) 'Macroeconomic Adjustment to Interest Rate Disturbances: Real and Monetary Aspects', in E. Claassen and P. Salin, (eds), *Recent Issues in the Theory of Flexible Exchange Rates*, North-Holland, Amsterdam.

KRUGMAN, P. (1988) 'Long-run Effects of the Strong Dollar', in R. C. Martson (ed.), *Misalignment of Exchange Rates: Effects on Trade and Industry*, Chicago University Press, Chicago, Ill.

McKINNON, R. (1976) 'The Limited Role of Fiscal Policy in an Open Economy', *Banca Nazionale del Lavoro Quarterly Review*, Rome.

MEADE, J. (1979) 'Notes on "Fiscal and Monetary Policies in an Open Economy" by M. Fetherston and W. Godley', mimeo, Department of Applied Economics, Cambridge.

MURATA, Y. (1977) *Mathematics for Stability and Optimization of Economic Systems*, Academic Press, New York.

MUSSA, M. (1986) 'The Effects of Commercial, Fiscal, Monetary, and

Exchange Rate Policies on the Real Exchange Rate', in S. Edwards and L. Ahamaed (eds), *Economic Adjustment and Exchange Rates in Developing Countries*, University of Chicago Press, Chicago, IL.

PURVIS, D. (1985) 'Public Sector Deficits, International Capital Movements, and the Domestic Economy: The Medium-term is the message', *Canadian Journal of Economics*, no. 4, pp. 723–42.

RODRIGUEZ, C. (1979) 'Short and Long-run Effects of Monetary and Fiscal Policies under Flexible Exchange Rates and Perfect Capital Mobility', *American Economic Review*, vol. 69 (March), pp. 176–82.

SACHS, J. (1980) 'Wages, Flexible Exchange Rates, and Macroeconomic Policy', *Quarterly Journal of Economics*, vol. 94, (June), pp. 731–47.

SACHS, J. and WYPLOSZ, C. (1984) 'Real Exchange Rate Effects of Fiscal Policy', National Bureau of Economic Research, Working Paper no. 1255 (January), Cambridge, MA.

SARGENT, T. (1979) *Macroeconomic Theory*, Academic Press, New York.

SERVEN, L. (1990) 'Anticipated Real Exchange-Rate Changes and the Dynamics of Investment', World Bank Working Paper WPS562 (December), Washington, DC.

SOLOW, R. (1983) 'Comment' on W. Godley, 'Keynes and the Management of Real National Income and Expenditure', in D. Worswick and J. Trevithick (eds), *Keynes and the Modern World*, Cambridge University Press, Cambridge.

TOBIN, J. (1982) 'Money and Finance in the Macroeconomic Process', *Journal of Money, Credit and Banking*, vol. 14, no. 2 (May).

TOBIN, J. and BRAGA DE MACEDO, J. (1980) 'The Short-Run Macro-economics of Floating Exchange Rates: An Exposition', in J. S. Chipman and C. P. Kindleberger (eds), *Flexible Exchange Rates and the Balance of Payments*, North-Holland, Amsterdam, pp. 5–28.

TOBIN, J. and BUITER, W. (1976) 'Long-run Effects of Fiscal and Monetary Policy on Aggregate Demand', in J. Stein (ed), *Monetarism*, North-Holland, Amsterdam.

TURNOVSKY, S. (1976) 'The Dynamics of Fiscal Policy in an Open Economy', *Journal of International Economics*, vol. 6 (May).

TURNOVSKY, S. (1977) *Macroeconomic Analysis and Stabilization Policies*, Cambridge University Press, Cambridge.

WHITTAKER, R. S. *et al.* (1986) 'Alternative Financial Policy Rules in an Open Economy under Rational and Adaptative Expectations', *Economic Journal*, vol. 96.

WILSON, C. (1979) 'Exchange Rate Dynamics and Anticipated Disturbances', *Journal of International Economics* (June).

Index

Absorption approach to the balance of
    payments 19
Aggregate supply 9

Capital gains and losses 39

Disposable income effect 42, 43, 50,
    85
Distributed lag models 94
    of GDP 100
    of privately held financial
      assets 98
Dornbusch model 25
Dornbusch and Fischer model 6, 32
Downward-flexible real wage 11, 19

Financial markets 38, 79, 81–2
Fiscal deficits 40, 44, 65
Fiscal policy
    and real wage rigidity 29
    rules 7, 37, 72
Flow relationships 36, 76
Forward-looking expectations 30, 36

Goods market adjustment 36, 55, 80

Impact adjustment
    of exchange rate 53
    of goods market 58
Interest earnings on foreign assets 1,
    3, 6
Interest rate
    covered parity condition 39
    impact effects 54
    long-run changes in response to
      foreign interest variations 24

IS–LM model 94

Keynes, *General Theory* 87

Long-run multipliers
    of domestic public debt on
      exchange rate 24, 44

Harrod trade multiplier of foreign
    trade 18
    of public expenditure on GDP 15,
      17, 27
    of public expenditure on privately
      held financial assets 13

Mean lag
    of GDP towards its long-run
      equilibrium 101
    precursors of mean lag results 104
    of privately held financial assets
      towards its long-run
      equilibrium 98.
    Solow criticisms 110
Medium-run multiplier of public
    expenditure on GDP 90–2
Monetary approach to the balance of
    payments 68, 97
Money market adjustment 40, 44
Monotonic convergence path
    of exchange rate 51–3
    of GDP 90
Mundell–Fleming model with a
    supply side 4
Mundell–Fleming propositions 1, 8
    Branson and Buiter
      amendments 7, 16
    Frenkel and Razin version 2, 8, 17
    Sachs criticism 2, 15
    Sachs and Wyplosz version 32, 52

Non-monotonic convergence path
    conditions to rule out 109
    of exchange rate 33, 34, 58–60
    of GDP 109

Overshooting of long-term
    equilibrium of GDP 109–112

Private savings 5, 8, 31
Privately held financial assets
    changes due to increase in domestic
      public debt 46
    long-run desired level 43

Productivity
  of labor   4, 9
  in tradable sector   33

Real consumption wage   9
Real wage rigidity   2, 20
  Branson and Rotemberg model   9, 10
  Dreze and Modigliani model   10
Risk-premium   39, 48

Short-run multiplier of public
  expenditure on GDP   87, 93

Speed of adjustment
  of GDP toward its long-run
    equilibrium   88
  of privately held financial
    assets   97
Stability conditions
  of a model with predetermined
    variables   112
  saddle point properties of a model
    with non-predetermined
    variables   34, 60, 62
Stock relationships   79
Stock–flow relationships   42

Walras' law   82

WIDENER UNIVERSITY
WOLFGRAM
LIBRARY
CHESTER, PA.